The Rhythmic Psalter:

The book of Psalms squeezed into ten verse packages.

CANON SUE WALLACE

Copyright © 2020 Sue Wallace

All rights reserved.

ACKNOWLEDGEMENTS

I am very grateful to the trustees of the Transcendence charity for releasing my time to write this psalter. Thanks are also due to Malcolm Wallace, Kate Jones, Mike Griffiths, Richard Horton, Paula Horton, and Judith Pope who helped me immensely by proofreading and making suggestions for improvements. I'm also grateful to all those musicians, composers, liturgists, priests, artists and poets who have inspired me over the years by composing beautiful psalm settings. Last, and most importantly, I owe my grateful thanks to the glorious Trinity; source of all our life and inspiration.

INTRODUCTION

The journey which inspired this collection of 150 short psalms began in 2010 when I moved to Leeds Minster. The church at that time had a shortened fifteen minute version of morning prayer every day, and often used a shortened psalm within this service. However, there weren't many of these psalms and I made a resolution to edit a few more to use in order to give some variety. In my psalm edits I tried to convey a sense of the whole journey of the psalm within ten brief verses but I put down the task after a few months. Eventually I picked up the text in 2019 because I was concerned that the psalms were simply not being used enough in public worship. This diminishes both our biblical knowledge and our vocabulary in prayer. I wanted to help churches to learn different and creative ways of using these wonderful texts.

This was when I realised that what was actually needed was a more rhythmic psalter that could be used in churches where bands, drum circles and percussion are used to accompany the worship. This is why the texts have very tight rhythms in this collection. I also hope that the strong rhythms within these psalms will help those who read them to memorise some of the texts so that they can carry them with them throughout their daily lives. Although these psalms have suggested rhythms written in music notation as a guideline many of these psalms will work with different rhythmic patterns, so do feel free to experiment. One problem that I had whilst writing this psalter is that some words can be set to a number of different rhythms (eg. heaven, violence or glorious); in these cases I have used dashes to indicate how to split the word, and an apostrophe, (ruin'd), or an underline, (Z<u>io</u>n), if it is to be said on one syllable.

I must also add a confession to this introduction. I am not a Hebrew scholar, but I did study several translations of the psalms which stick very closåely to the Hebrew whilst writing this book. Due to the rhythmic constraints of my task, some of these psalm verses have inevitably had to be paraphrases. I have used the Anglican numbering of the psalms and the verse numbers within this book so that readers (if they wish) can look up the more 'traditional' version within the Common Worship psalter which is freely available online. Not all these short psalms start at the first verse as sometimes the sense of the psalm can be better conveyed by starting somewhere in the middle of a lengthy psalm. I cannot aim to properly do justice to every psalm within a mere ten verses, and in the case of psalm 78 I really felt that I had to write another ten verses to make a second section. Psalm 119, however, despite its length, is consistent in its theme declaring the blessings of God's law.

I do hope that you will use this book creatively and the texts come with full permission to photocopy, project or disseminate the texts within an act of divine worship. and permission for musicians to create their own tunes to the texts if they feel inspired to do so. Do let me know if you have written one of these. I would love to hear it. I have a Rhythmic Psalter Youtube channel

https://bit.ly/rhythmic_psalter

which demonstrates a few examples of some different ways you can use these psalms but I am sure there are many more.

Sue Wallace February 2020 (SDG)

ACCOMPANIMENTS AND MUSICAL IDEAS

The psalms within this psalter are set to a number of different time signatures: 2/4, 6/8, 3/4 and 4/4. A tactic that seems to work well when playing these in church with percussion is if some of the congregation play one simple rhythmic pattern as an accompaniment (led by a confident drummer), and others play another, whilst the psalm is said or drummed. Trained musicians, if they wish, can improvise a bass line or some chords underneath the psalm. Chord sequences can be borrowed from hymns or worship songs, and talented drummers can add complex cross rhythms. You can also play beats and samples from the computer if you wish, although it can be difficult to get a congregation to properly keep time with these. It is also helpful before you start playing a psalm to explain how you are going to end the drumming.

Inviting the congregation to raise their hands when the conductor raises theirs is an excellent way of ending a period of drumming, as it is physically impossible to hit a drum with your hands remaining in the air! In less-formal situations I do warm-up elimination games with groups when I "conduct"; growing-taller for louder and crouching-down for growing-quieter before raising hands at random moments to stop the players. Those still playing when my hands are raised are "out" until there is a winner. This method often results in really close watching of the conductor as people are naturally quite competitive in elimination games!

In this following section of the book I have added some simple suggestions for rhythmic accompaniments but there are many others which can be used, depending on the skill of your drummers. The 6/8 rhythmic patterns can be used for any of the 6/8 psalms and adapted for the 3/4 psalms. Likewise the 2/4 patterns can be used for any of these, and also adapted for 4/4 psalms.

When explaining rhythms to a congregation it is really helpful to use simple words of phrases that people can recite in their heads (or perhaps say aloud!). You can change these to fit the psalm. For the example rhythm pattern below (6/8 pattern 1), the kick drum could be playing a heartbeat rhythm "ba-boom", the mid-pitched percussion could be playing "save-us, help-us", the high-pitched percussion could be playing "kings of the Earth take heed" and the shakers could be playing "Save us Lord, help us Lord".

Another tip is to think carefully about who gets which instrument. Only put loud instruments (such as tambourines and woodblocks) in the hands of people who have a good sense of rhythm. Give shakers or even rainsticks to people who have problems with their timing. Distributing deeper sounding instruments such as bass drums and larger djembes to good musicians can undergird the playing and help everyone keep to time. Spread these around the room (in a circle I tend to put them at the 4 quarter points).

The following sets of accompaniments are merely suggestions. Please do experiment and change instruments and rhythms if you wish. Sometimes you may wish to confine yourself to two simple rhythmic patterns as an accompaniment, especially with a smaller group.

RHYTHMIC PATTERNS FOR PSALMS IN 6/8 TIME

6/8 PATTERN 1

6/8 PATTERN 2

6/8 PATTERN 3

6/8 PATTERN 4

by Mike Griffiths

RHYTHMIC PATTERNS FOR PSALMS IN 2/4 TIME

2/4 PATTERN 1

2/4 PATTERN 2

2/4 PATTERN 3

2/4 PATTERN 4

RHYTHMIC PATTERNS FOR PSALMS IN 3/4 TIME

3/4 PATTERN 1

3/4 PATTERN 2

3/4 PATTERN 3

3/4 PATTERN 4

RHYTHMIC PATTERNS FOR PSALMS IN 4/4 TIME

4/4 PATTERN 1

4/4 PATTERN 2

4/4 PATTERN 3

4/4 PATTERN 4

SINGING A PSALM FROM THIS PSALTER

Although I originally envisaged that these psalms could be said rhythmically, rapped or drummed, they can also be chanted or sung. Because the rhythm is exact for each psalm "pointing" the notes (i.e. fitting them to the music) is easier than usual. Here I have given you some very simple tunes that can be used to chant the psalms. Do feel free to experiment, to try different methods and unusual instruments such as Boomwhackers or the tongue drum; write new tunes, interweave them with hymns or worship songs and sing a new song to God.

AN EASY DESCENDING CHANT
I have given guitar chords to accompany this chant.

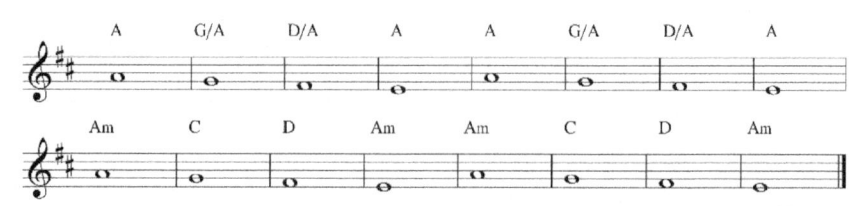

Line one of the music is the first line of psalm text, line two of the music is the second line of psalm text (etc).

AN EASY CHANT IN G MINOR

Once again I have added guitar chords. This music is enough for two lines of text. You can give added complexity by moving from the B flat to the G on some words and from the G to a low D on others. I demonstrate this technique with Psalm 90 on the Rhythmic Psalter Youtube channel.

First line of psalm text,   **second line of text.**

PLAINCHANT PSALM TONES

There are eight traditional plainchant psalm tones which were used in monasteries in the Middle Ages. These are still very popular today. Here I have given you the music to tone 8 which I think is the loveliest of the tones.

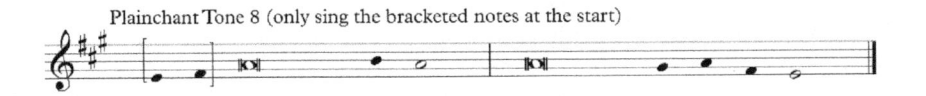

Plainchant Tone 8 (only sing the bracketed notes at the start)

The music to the others is easily available for free on the internet. One bar of this chant equals one line of text. You may also wish to experiment by using these psalms with different types of chant such as Anglican chant, or interspersing the words of the psalm with a chanted response in the form of a worship song or chant from the Taizé community in France.

Psalm 1

1 Bless-éd are those who've not walked with the wicked,
nor lingered within the way of the sinners,
nor sat within the collection of scornful.

2 These ones delight in the law of the Lord God.
They think on his law all day and at night-time.

3 Like the trees planted by streams of bright water
evergreen leaves bearing fruit in due season,
whatever they do, it prospers and then grows.

4 As for the wicked, it's not so with these ones;
they are like chaff blown away by a strong wind.

5 Therefore the wicked won't stand in the judgement,
nor sinners stand in the just-ones assembly.

6 For the Lord watches the way of the righteous,
but God destroys the cru'l ways of the wicked.

Psalm 2

1 O why are the nations in chaos?
Why do people make schemes together?

2 The kings of the earth are conspiring
upon the Lord and his anointed.

4 Our God who dwells high in the hea-vens
shall laugh at them, scorn them and mock them.

5 He'll speak to them in his great anger.
He'll terrify them with his fury.

6 'Yet I have appointed my own king
on Zi-on, my great holy mountain

7 I will proclaim the laws of my Lord;
he said : 'This day you are my son now;
this day I've become your own father.

8 If you ask in prayer I'll give nations.
The ends of the earth, they will be yours.'

10 And now, kings of earth, act with wisdom!
Take warning, earth's po-wer-ful rulers.

11 Serve God, kiss his feet with devotion.
12 They're happy, those with God as refuge.

Psalm 3

1 Lord I have so many enemies;
they are many who rise against me.

2 Many are they who say to my soul,
'There is no help for you in your God.'

3 O Lord God, you're a shield round my life;
you're my glory, you lift up my head.

4 When I cry loudly before my Lord,
then he answers from his holy hill;

5 I lie down sleeping and then I rise,
because my Lord God cares for my life.

6 I will not fear crowds of thousands now
those surrounding me on every side .

7 Rise now O Lord God and save my life,
strike my foes on the cheek, break their teeth!

8 Our whole salvation belongs to God:
On your people may your blessing fall.

Psalm 4

1 Hear me when I call my righteous God;
you freed me, have mercy, hear my prayer,

2 How long will you hurt my glor-ious name;
have pleasure in vanity and lies?

3 God works wonders for his faithful ones;
I call upon God, he answers me.

4 Now stand in your awe, and do not sin;
search your heart in bed and then be still.

5 In right-eous-ness offer sacrifice.
put your trust in God, trust in the Lord.

6 Some people say, 'Who will show us good?'
Yet your good face shines light down on us.

7 You put joy in my heart and much more,
more than wine and oil and corn bring joy.

8 In holy peace I lie down and sleep,
for you keep me safely, O my Lord.

Psalm 5

1 Give ear to my words, O Lord my God;
listen to all my laments and sighs.

2 Hear all my crying, my King, my God,
For to you Lord I will make my prayer.

3 Lord, in the morning, you will hear me;
as morning dawns I will raise my head.

4 You have no delight in wrong-do-ing;
for evil cannot live in your house.

5 The proud cannot stand within your sight
and you despise all the wrongdo-ers.

6 You destroy those who speak out their lies;
bloodthirsty li-ars the Lord detests.

7 But as for me, through your great mercy,
I'll come and bow to your temple's throne.

8 Lead me, O Lord, in your right-eous-ness;
make your way straight now before my face.

12 Let those who hide in you now be glad;
let them sing out for joy evermore.

14 Lord, you will favour and bless the just;
you'll cover them like a crown or shield.

Psalm 6

1 Lord, don't rebuke me in your anger;
or discipline me in your rage.

2 Have mercy on me, for I am weak;
Lord heal me, my bones are in pain.

3 My soul also shakes in great terror;
how long, O Lord, tell me how long?

4 Turn now, and deliver my soul, Lord
 and save me for your mercy's sake.

5 For in death no-one can recall you;
and who gives you thanks in the grave?

6 I'm weary at night with my groaning;
I flood my night pillow with tears.

7 My eyes are tired, wasted with grieving,
and worn away due to my foes.

8 Depart from me, you that do evil
my weeping is heard by the Lord.

9 God hears all my pleading and praying;
my God will receive all my prayers.

10 My en-e-mies are shamed and shaken;
they shall turn back in their great shame.

Psalm 7

1 O Lord my God, I take refuge in you;
Save me from my persecutors. Rescue me!

2 Lest they maul me like beasts tearing my flesh,
and drag me away with no-one to save me.

3 O Lord my God, if I have done these things:
if there's wickedness or guilt within my hands,

4 if I have paid my friends back with evil,
or I've robbed my enemy without a cause,

5 then let my en-e-my overtake me,
trample me and lay my honour in the dust.

9 Defend the righteous and end wicked ways,
for you test the mind and heart, O righteous God!

10 God is a shield of protection round me;
God will save the true, those upright in their hearts.

14 Look at those who labour at wickedness,
they're pregnant with trouble, they give birth to lies.

16 The trouble they make for others backfires;
their vio-lence will come back down upon their heads.

17 I will thank the Lord for his righteousness,
I'll make music to my God, the Lord Most High.

Psalm 8

1 O Lord God our go-ver-nor, your name is great,
how glo-ri-ous is your name in all the world!

2 Your majesty above the hea-vens is praised.
It's praised from the mouths of young babes at the breast.

3 You've strengthened your po-wer against all your foes,
your enemies' vengeance you can then make still.

4 When I see the hea-vens, the work of your hands,
the moon and the starscape which you have arranged,

5 then what are mere mortals, that you care for us;
these mere human beings, that you seek us out?

6 We're made a touch lower than your angel host,
encircled with honour and with glory crowned.

7 You made them rule over the works of your hands,
all things that exist you place under their feet,

8 The sheep and the oxen, the beasts of the field,
9 the birds of the air and the fish in the sea,
and all things that move in the paths of the sea.

10 O Lord God our governor, your name is great
  how glo-ri-ous is your name in all the world!

Psalm 9

1 I give thanks to you my God, with my whole heart;
I will tell of your marvellous works.

2 O let me rejoice, let me be glad in you.
I'll make music to your name, Most High.

3 When all of my enemies are driven back,
for they stumble and fall at your sight.

4 For you have maintained my right and helped my cause;
and you sat enthroned as a wise judge.

5 You chastised the nations, the wicked destroyed,
and you wiped out their names ever more.

6 The enemy's finished, eternally ruin'd.
You uprooted their cities from earth.

7 But God reigns forever, is always enthroned;
as a judge he has set up his throne.

8 He will judge the world with his justice and truth
and rule nations with true honesty.

9 God will be a shelter for all the oppressed,
and a refuge within troubled times.

10 And those who do know your name will trust in you,
you will not forsake those who seek you.

Psalm 10

1 Now why do you stand so far off, O my Lord?
And why hide yourself when times of trouble come?

2 The arrogant wicked persecute the poor;
now let them be caught by their own wicked plans.

3 The wicked will boast of their own heart's desire;
the co-ve-tous curse God and insult his name.

4 In arrogance they say 'God will not avenge';
within all their scheming there's no room for God.

10 The lowly are broken, stooping before them;
the helpless are crushed beneath the wicked's power.

11 They say in their hearts, 'God has forgotten us;
he conceals his face, he will not see our deeds'.

12 Arise O my God, and lift your mighty hand;
forget not the poor, don't let them be ignored.

17 The Lord is now king, and shall reign ever more;
and all Godless nations vanish from the land.

18 O Lord you will hear the crying of the poor;
you will hear their cries, you will strengthen their hearts.

19 You give justice to the orphans and oppressed,
so people no longer run from terror's hand.

Psalm 11

1 I hide and take refuge in my God;
how then can you say before my face,
'Go fly like a bird, and seek the hills.'

2 Now see how the wicked bend their bows.
They fit their sharp arrows to the string,
to hide and shoot at the true of heart.

3 When all the foundations are destroyed,
what can those who love God's justice do?

4 The Lord in his holy temple dwells;
God has made the hea-vens as his throne.

5 His eyes look down and behold the world,
his gaze probes through every human heart.

6 God judges the just with wicked ones,
yet those who love vi-o-lence he hates.

7 He sends burning sulphur on the vile;
he punishes them with scorching wind.

8 For our God is just and loves just deeds;
and those who are upright see his face.

Psalm 12

1 God, help me, there's no-one godly left;
the faithful have vanished from our human race.

2 They speak lies, they lie to those nearby;
with their lips they flatter, but their hearts tell lies.

3 O that God would end the flattering lips
and tongues that would utter out vile, boastful, words!

4 Those who say, 'With our words we'll prevail;
our lips we will use, who is Lord over us?'

5 'Poor people are crushed, the needy groan.
I will rise up now,' says God, 'To rescue them.'

6 Your words Lord, are pure and holy words,
like silver in fi-re, purified seven times.

7 You, O God, will keep watch over us
and guard us from this fierce generation now.

8 Guard, although the wicked stride about,
and evil's exalted by the human race.

Psalm 13

1 How long will you forget me God; for ever?
How long will you hide your bright face from me?

2 How long shall I grieve, with anguish in my heart?
How long shall my e-ne-my walk on me?

3 Look on me and answer, O God my saviour;
give light to my eyes, or I'll sleep in death;

4 While enemies say, 'I have overcome him,'
and my foes rejoice, rejoice at my fall.

5 But as for me, I'll trust your loving mercy.
My heart will rejoice in your saving name.

6 I will sing to God, my Lord and my Saviour,
for he has dealt ge-ne-rously with me.

Psalm 14

1 The fools in their hearts say that there is no God.
Their actions are evil, and they are corrupt;
there's no-one that does good, no, not even one.

2 God looks down upon all the children of earth,
to see if wise people are seeking out God.

3 But everyone has turned back, all are corrupt:
there's no-one that does good; no, not even one.

4 Do they not have knowledge, these ones who do wrong?
These wicked-ones eat up my people like bread.
They'll never call out, never cry out to God.

5 But they will then tremble, they'll be terror-filled;
God dwells with the just and lives with righteous ones.

6 The wicked ones frustrate the plans of the poor,
yet God shelters them, he will be their refuge.

7 O that Isr-ael's saving help would come from Zion!
At God's freedom, Jacob and Is-rael rejoice.

Psalm 15

1 Lord, who may dwell in your sacred tent?
And who may rest on your holy hill?

2 Whoever leads a good, blameless life
and always does what is good and right;

who speaks the truth from a sincere heart
3 who does not slander or speak deceit;

4 Who does no evil thing to their friend;
who does not slur or scorn their neighbour;

5 those who despise vile and wicked ones,
yet honours those ones who fear the Lord.

6 Whoever has sworn to their neighbour
who never goes back upon their word;

7 who does not lend cash in hope of gain,
who takes no bribes, whose words can't be bought.

8 Whoever does these things shall stand firm;
they'll never stumble, they shall not fall.

Psalm 16

1 Preserve me, O God, I take refuge in you;
I say 'Lord my God, goodness all comes from you.'

2 My heroes are the godly ones in the land,
I take joy in all of the noble in heart.

3 Though idols are many, and crowds follow them,
I will not take part in their offerings of blood,
I will not make mention of their unclean names.

4 The Lord God himself is my portion and cup;
you safeguard my future in your hands alone

5 and green, pleasant places are marked out for me;
a good, pleasing heritage is indeed mine.

6 I will bless the Lord who has counselled my life,
and in the night watches he speaks to my heart.

7 I will keep God always before me in life;
with God at my right hand, then I shall not fall.

8 My spirit rejoices and my heart is glad;
my body is safe now when it takes its rest.

9 You will not leave me in the realm of the dead,
nor leave your be-lov-ed one down in the pit.

10 You'll show me the path of life; fullness of joy
and in your right hand is joy for evermore.

Psalm 17

1 Hear my just cause Lord, now heed my complaint;
I'm not deceitful, Lord, answer my prayer.

2 Let my acquittal come forth from your throne;
let your eyes look at the true and the right.

3 Look at my heart as you visit by night.
Refine me, you'll find no wrongdo'ng in me.

6 I call on you Lord, you'll answer I know;
bend down your ear to me, hear all my words.

7 Saving the shelterers at your right hand,
 show me your marv-el-lous kindness and love,

8 Keep me now as the apple of your eye;
hide me beneath the shade of your great wings.

9 Hide from those wicked and their assaults,
en-e-mies surround me to steal my life.

10 They've closed their hearts to compassion and love;
their mouths speak out in their proud arrogance.

13 Arise Lord, confront them, cast them all down;
save me from wickedness, save by your sword.

16 As for me, in goodness I'll see your face;
when I wake and see you I'll be content.

Psalm 18

1 I love you, my Lord, you are my strength.
My rock, and my fort, you save me.

2 My God is my rock and my refuge,
my shield, my salvation, my tow'r.

3 I cried to the Lord in my anguish,
and see, I am saved from my foes.

5 The chords of the pit fastened round me;
the tangles of death curled round me.

6 In my anguish I called upon God.
I cried out to my God for help.

7 He heard all my prayers from his temple
and my cries were heard by his ears.

10 He parted the hea-vens and came down;
thick darkness was under his feet.

11 He climbed on the cherubim and flew;
he soared on the wings of the wind.

12 A brightness shone out from before him,
with hailstones and flashes of fire.

20 He brought us to new lands of freedom;
he rescued me in his delight.

Psalm 19

1 The hea-vens are telling the glory of God;
the skies all display his craftsmanship.

2 For day after day they continue to speak,
and night after night they make him known.

3 They speak without sound, and they speak without word,
and so their qui'et voices are not heard,

4 yet their message goes out to all of the lands
and their words go into the whole world.

5 In hea-ven he sets up a tent for the sun,
that comes like a bridegroom from out of his room
with joy like a champion in a race.

6 From one end of sky running up to the next,
there is nothing hidden from its heat.

7 God's law is quite perfect, reviving the soul;
God's word is quite firm, it makes fools wise.

8 God's statutes are right and give joy to the heart;
God's laws ever sure, they light the eyes.

9 God's fear is quite pure and it lives ever more;
God's judgements are true, each one is fair.

10 More precious than gold, even than much fine gold,
they're sweeter than honey, from the comb.

Psalm 20

1 May God hear you in days of trouble,
the name of Jacob's God defend you;

2 may he send you help from his temple
and strengthen you from out of Zi-on;

3 may he remember all your offerings,
and accept all of your burnt offerings;

4 may he grant all your heart's desires;
may he make all your plans successful.

5 May we rejoice in your salvation
and triumph in the name of our God;
may God now answer all your pray-ers.

6 Now I know God saves his anointed;
he'll answer from his holy hea-ven,
he'll answer with his mighty right hand.

7 Some trust in char-i-ots and horses,
but we will put our trust in our God.

8 Those nations will collapse and fall down,
we will rise up and we will stand firm.

9 Give vic-tory to our King O Lord God,
and answer when we call upon you.

Psalm 21

1 The king shall rejoice in your strength, O God;
How greatly he rejoices in your victories!

2 You have given to him his heart's desire.
You have not denied any requests of his lips.

3 You welcomed him with blessings of goodness
and you set a crown of finest gold on his head.

4 He asked of you life, you gave it to him,
the days of his life, they stretch on forever more.

5 His honour is great through your saving help;
with glory you clothed him, you gave him majesty.

6 You've granted him happiness evermore.
You will make him glad filled with joy in your presence.

7 Our king, he puts his trust within the Lord;
the kindness of God will keep him from be-ing moved.

8 Your hand shall mark down all your enemies;
your strong right hand will seize all those who hate your name.

12 For you will force them to retreat and leave
when you aim at them with your bow, the arrows poised.

13 Rise up, O Lord, rise in your might and power,
with music and with singing we praise your great acts.

Psalm 22

1 My God, my God, O why have you forsaken me,
why so far from salvation,
From the words of my distress?

2 I cry all day Lord, but you do not answer me;
and throughout the night season I find I cannot take rest.

3 O Holy One, enthroned on praise from Israel.
4 Our forebears trusted in your name;
they trusted, you saved them.

5 But as for me, I am a worm and not a man,
I'm scorned by all, detested by all people who see me.

6 He trusted God, and so let God deliver him;
and so let him deliver him, if he delights in him.

16 My enemies surround me like a pack of dogs;
an evil gang crowds in on me, they pierce my hands and feet.

17 I count my bones; my enemies they stare and gloat.
18 They cast lots for my robes and split my clothes up among them.

19 But O my God, I beg you be not far from me;
you are my greatest strength,
please hasten, hasten to help me.

22 I will declare your name to all my family;
from in the middle of the congregation, I'll praise you.

Psalm 23

1 The Lord is my shepherd; I shall not want.
2 He makes me lie down in green pastures.
He leads me beside the still waters.

3 My life he brings back, he renews my soul
and guides me in pathways of goodness;
he guides me for his holy name's sake.

4 And though I walk through the valley of death
and valley of shadows I shan't fear;

for you are with me, and your rod and staff,
your rod and staff they bring me comfort.

5 You prepare a table before my eyes
in the presence of my attackers.

And you have anointed my head with oil
and my cup is now overflowing.

6 For now surely goodness shall follow me
and mercy each day of my lifespan.
I'll dwell in God's house now for ever.

Psalm 24

1 The Earth is God's and everything in it,
the world and all those who dwell within.

2 He set it firmly founded on the seas
and on the deep rivers made it firm.

3 Who shall ascend the hill of the Lord God,
and who shall stand in his holy place.

4 The ones who have clean hands and a pure heart.
Who have not made idols or false oaths.

5 They shall receive a blessing from our God,
and gain treasure from the God who saves.

6 This is the generation of searchers,
who seek out your face O Jacob's God.

7 Lift up your heads you gates, O be lifted.
Be lifted you everlasting doors;
and our king of glory shall come in.

8 Who is this king? This glo-ri-ous ruler?
The Lord, strong upon the battlefield.

9 Lift up your heads you gates, O be lifted.
Be lifted you everlasting doors
and our king of glory shall come in.

10 Who is this king? This glo-ri-ous ruler?
The Lord, strong upon the battlefield.

Psalm 25

1 To you O Lord I lift up my soul;
O my God, my trust is in you.

Lord let me never be put to shame;
nor let my en-e-mies triumph.

2 Let no-one who seeks you be ashamed,
but shame and frustrate the traitors.

3 Let me know your ways, teach me your paths,
4 guide me in your truth and teach me.

The God of my salvation is you.
In you I hope all the day long.

5 Remember Lord compassion and love
for they are from everlasting.

6 Remember not the sins of my youth
but think of me in your goodness.

7 How upright, gracious, is our Lord God;
so shall he teach sinners God's way.

8 He'll guide the humble in doing right
and teach his ways to the lowly.

9 The ways of God are mercy and truth
to those who keep his commandments.

Psalm 26

1 Give judgement for my integrity;
I've trusted in God without wavering.

2 Examine me Lord God, and try me;
now test out my mind, audit my heart.

3 For I'm conscious of your endless love;
and I walk in your truthful pathway.

4 I do not spend my time with the liars,
I shall not walk with the deceitful.

5 I hate gath-er-ings of evil do'ers
I'll not take my seat with the wicked.

6 I will wash my hands in innocence
that I may encircle your altar,

7 to sing out a song of thankful praise
and tell of your marvels and wonders.

8 Lord I love your house, your temple house,
the place with your glory abiding.

9 Don't sweep me away with sinful souls,
do not condemn me with the mur-d'rers.

11 Yet I will walk with integrity;
redeem me God, have mercy on me.

Psalm 27

1 The Lord is my light and my saving help;
so who on earth shall I fear?
The Lord is the strength, the strength of my life;
I will not be afraid now.

2 When enemies come to eat up my flesh
they stumble and they fall down.

3 Though hosts of attackers camp nearby me,
my strong heart will not fear them.
And though war breaks out, breaks out against me,
I'll put my trust in my God.

4 One thing have I asked of God, that I seek:
to live in God's house always.

5 To gaze on the radiant beauty of God;
to seek him in his temple.

6 In my days of trouble he'll shelter me;
he'll hide me under his tent,
he'll set me high on a rock.

7 And now he will lift my head, raised up high
above my foes around me;

8 and therefore I offer glad sacrifice;
my heart makes music to God.

9 O hear my voice, Lord, O hear when I call;
have mercy on me, answer.

10 My heart speaks to me and says 'Seek his face.'
Your face, O Lord, will I seek.

Psalm 28

1 To you Lord I call, Lord God my rock;
Lord don't be deaf to my crying,
or I shall fall, like those in the pit
if you are silent before me.

2 O hear my prayer's voice, Lord when I cry
I lift my hands to your temple.

3 Do not drag me down, with evil ones
who speak of peace to their neighbours,
but they have malice in their hearts.

4 Repay them for those deeds they have done
for all their scheming and evil.

6 For they pay no heed to our Lord's deeds;
they brush off the work of his hands.
And therefore our God shall break them down,
They shall not ever be rebuilt.

7 O blest be the Lord, blest be the Lord;
he has heard my cry for mercy.

8 The Lord is my strength, God is my shield,
my trust is in him, my helper.

9 And therefore my heart dances for joy;
my songs will be songs of praises.

10 The Lord is the strength of his nation,
a shelter for his anointed.

11 Lord save your people, bless your estate,
shepherd them, carry them always.

Psalm 29

1 Honour the Lord, you hea-ven-ly beings,
honour his strength and his glory proclaim.

2 Honour the Lord, for his name's pure glory;
worship in beauty and in holiness.

3 The voice of God resounds on the waters;
the voice of God, in his glory, thunders;
the Lord upon the immense water flood.

4 The voice of God is a mighty utter-ance;
the voice of God is a glo-ri-ous voice.

5 The voice of God can fracture the Cedars;
the voice of God shatters Lebanon's trees.

6 Lebanon he makes skip like a young calf,
Sirion dancing like oxen at play.

7 The voice of God spits flashes of lightning;
the voice of God makes the wilderness shake;

the voice of God shakes deserts in Kadesh.
8 **The voice of God makes the oaks twist and writhe.**

The voice of God strips strong forest branches;
in his great temple they cry 'Glor-ious God'

9 God sits upon his throne on the water;
God is enthroned as a king evermore.

10 Our God will give his strength to his people,
God will then bless all his people with peace.

Psalm 30

1 I'll praise you O Lord my God, for you have raised me up;
you have not let my oppressors triumph over me.

3 You have raised me up from death to life from the deep pit;
4 servants of God sing to him and give thanks to his name.

5 For his anger quickly goes, his blessings last a life.
Heaviness may last the night but joy comes with the dawn.

6 When I thrived and prospered I said 'I shall not be moved'.
O Lord when you favoured me,
you gave me mountain-strength.

7 Then you hid your face from me and I was heartbroken.
8 O my Lord I called to you. I cried to God for help:

9 'What gain is there in my death If I sink in the pit.
Will the dust be praising you. Will it tell of your faith?'

10 Hear me God, have mercy now. Oh Lord God be my help.
11You have turned my tears to dancing; rags to clothes of joy.

12 So my heart will always sing, I'll never cease my song.
For all time I will thank you, I'll thank you ever more.

Psalm 31

1 In you, O my Lord, I've claimed refuge now;
Lord save me, let me not be shamed.

2 Turn your ear to me and listen to me;
come quickly to rescue me Lord.

3 Be my stronghold rock, a fort to save me,
for your name's sake guide and lead me.

4 Take me from the trap my enemies set,
you are my protection and strength.

5 I entrust my spirit into your hand,
redeeming me, Lord God of truth.

15 My times and my future are in your hand;
save me from my enemies' grasp,

16 O make your face shine on your servant now,
and save me for your mercy's sake.

17 'Don't leave me disgraced, O Lord God' I plead,
I call to you my Lord for help;

but let all the wicked be put to shame;
And let them lie still in the grave.

18 Let their lying lips be silenced by you
that speak with disdain and contempt.

19 How great and how lavish your goodness, Lord,
which you hide for those who fear you;
which you have prepared in everyone's sight
on those who take refuge in you.

Psalm 32

1 Happy the people who sins are forgiven,
whose sins are covered and wrongdoings wiped.

2 What joy for those ones God has cleared of their guilt,
those in whose spirit's there is no deceit.

3 When I would not confess my bones were wasting
through my great guilt, I groaned all the day long.

4 Your good hand, day and night, lay firmly on me;
my strength was dried, like a hot summer drought.

5 Then I acknowledged all my sins before you
and I stopped trying to hide all my guilt.

6 'I will confess all my wrongs to the Lord God'
and you forgave all the guilt of my sin.

7 The faithful will call you in times of trouble;
they will not drown within the water floods.

8 You are my safe place, you will keep me from harm.
You surround my life with salvation songs.

9 I will instruct you, I will show you your path,
and I will fix my eyes firmly on you.

10 Do not be senseless like young colts or donkeys
who need strong bridles to keep them controlled.

11 Troubles and sorrows will come to the wicked,
mercy surrounds those who trust in the Lord.

Psalm 33

1 Be happy in God, O you righteous,
It's right and good for the pure to sing his praise.

2 Make music to God on the ly-re;
on the ten stringed instrument sing him your songs.

3 Sing out to him now, sing a new song;
play skilfully to him with great shouts of praise.

4 For God's word is true and is faithful
and all of his works are trustworthy and sure.

5 Whatever is just and good he loves;
his endless compassion and love fills the world.

6 By God's word the hea-vens were fashioned;
he breathed out his word and the bright stars were born.

7 He gathers the sea in a great heap
and placed the great oceans in his treasure house.

20 We longingly wait for our Lord God;
for he is our helper and he is our shield.

21 For in him our hearts are rejoicing;
for we trust in his name, in his holy name.

22 May your kindness, Lord, be upon us,
because we have put all of our hope in you.

Psalm 34

1 I'll bless the Lord God at all times;
his praise shall ever be in my mouth.

2 My soul shall glory in the Lord;
let humble souls listen and be glad.

3 O magnify the Lord with me;
come let us together lift his name.

4 I looked for God, he answered me
he saved me from all my deepest fears.

5 Look on him, be aglow with joy,
no shadow of shame shall cross your face.

6 This poor soul cried, and God heard me;
God saved me in all my troubled times.

7 God's angel camps around the just
he encircles them and sets them free.

8 O taste and see, the Lord is good;
bless-éd is the one who trusts in him.

9 O Fear the Lord, you holy ones,
for those who fear him have all they need.

10 Li-ons may suffer hunger pangs,
but those who seek God lack nothing good.

Psalm 35

1 Contend O Lord with my contenders,
fight against those who fight against me.

2 Put on your armour, take up your shield,
rise to my aid 'God, my saving God'.

4 May those who seek me be put to shame;
those who plot ruin turn back in dismay.

5 Scatter them like chaff before the wind,
with God's great angel driving them down.

6 Let all their paths be slipp'ry and dark,
the Angel of the Lord chasing them.

7 They spread a trap for me without cause;
Without cause they dug pits for my soul.

8 Let ru-in come on them unawares;
let them be caught in the traps they laid;
let them fall to their own destruction.

9 Then will my soul be joyful in God
and I'll be glad for he rescues me.

10 My bones say 'Lord who is there like you?'
Who saves the poor from all wicked hands.

Psalm 36

1 Sin speaks to wicked ones within their hearts depths;
there's no respect for God within their eyes.

2 Their mouths are full of deceit, crime, and hatred;
they have stopped being wise or doing good.

5 Your love, O Lord, is as vast as the heav-ens
your faithfulness reaches beyond the clouds.

6 Your righteousness stands like these mighty mountains,
with justice you save both people and beasts.

7 How precious your love and mercy, O Lord God!
All flesh shall rest in the shade of your wings.

8 They shall be satisfied with your provision;
and they shall drink from your stream of delights.

9 You have the fountain of life everlasting
and in your ra-di-ance shall we see light.

10 Pour out your kindness to people who love you
and pour your justice on the true of heart.

11 Let not the proud of heart trample upon me
nor the ungodly's hands push me away.

12 They will all topple, all those who do evil.
They are thrown down, and they shall never rise.

Psalm 37

1 Do not fret because of evildoers;
don't be jealous of those who do wrong.

2 They shall all soon wither like the grasses,
like the spring flowers they will fade away.

3 Trust in God and do some good in your life;
dwell in this land, be nourished with truth.

4 Let your joy, your happiness be in God
and he will give you your heart's desires.

5 Give your path to God, put your trust in him,
trust him and he will bring it to pass.

6 He will make your justice clear as the light
and your just acts as the mid-day sun.

7 Be still before God and wait before him;
don't fear the rich who make evil plans.

8 Cease your anger and abandon your wrath;
don't fret, lest you're tempted to do wrong.

9 Evildoers? They shall all be cut off,
those who wait for God shall take the land.

10 In a while the wicked shall all be gone;
search for their place but they will be gone.

11 But the lowly shall possess the land then;
they'll delight in the fullness of peace.

Psalm 38

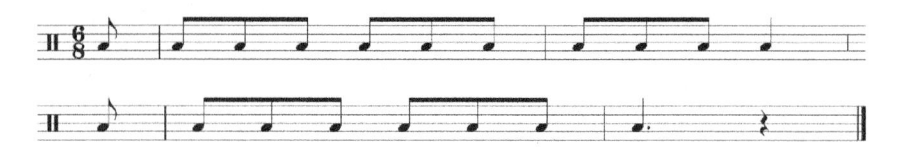

1 In all your displeasure don't punish me Lord,
or discipline me in your rage,

2 for all of your arrows have sunk into me;
your hand presses hard on my back.

3 Because of your anger my body is sick
and there is no health in my bones.

4 For all my wrong-do-ing has gone to my head;
my sins are too heavy to bear.

9 O Lord you know all of my secret desires,
my sighs are not hidden from you.

15 In you, O Lord my God, I will put my trust.
You will answer me, Lord my God.

16 I prayed 'Don't let enemies gloat over me,
rejoicing if my foot should slip.

17 I feel like I am on the edge of a cliff
and pain fills the whole of my life.

21 Lord do not forsake me, or stay far from me,
do not keep your distance, O Lord.

22 Come quickly to help me, come quickly to help.
O God of my salvation, come!'

Psalm 39

1 I said, 'I will keep watch over my ways,
that I might not sin with my tongue.

2 I will guard my mouth, and muzzle it shut
while those wicked are in my sight.'

5 Let me know my end and number of days,
how fleeting the span of my life.

6 My days short as hands, a blink in your sight;
the best of us are like a breath.

7 We walk round like shadows, hoarding in vain,
our riches unknown ones will spend.

8 And now, O my Lord, what do I wait for?
Lord my hope is found within you.

9 Lord save me from my wrongdoing and sins.
Don't let me be mocked by the fools.

11 Take your scourge away, your plague from my house;
I'm crushed by the blows from your hand.

12 We're punished, our beauty eaten by moths;
our lives last no longer than breath.

15 Turn your frown from me, that I may gain strength,
before I die, and breathe no more.

Psalm 40

1 My soul waited patiently for God;
he turned to me and he heard my cry.

2 He brought me up from the roaring pit,
and up from the mire and from the clay;
he set my feet firm upon a rock;
he made my weak footsteps firm and sure.

3 He has put a new song in my mouth,
a song singing praise before our God;
for many shall see and many fear
and so put their hope within the Lord.

4 How blest is the one who trusts in God,
not hailing the proud who follow lies.

5 How great are your doings O my Lord.
Great are your plans, no-one can compare!

6 If I were to tell, were to proclaim,
they would be more than I can express.

7 You do not need sacrifice or gifts
but you've opened up my deafened ears;

8 Our burnt offe-rings you do not re-quire;
then I said to my Lord 'Here, I come.

9 In your holy scroll it's written down
that I should do your will, my Lord God;
my joy is your law within my heart.'

10 I speak of you to the worshippers;
I speak of your faithfulness and help.

Psalm 41

1 Bless-éd are those who care for the poor;
God will save them in their troubled times.

2 God will give life, grant true happiness,
he shan't give them to their en'mies will.

3 God will help them on their bed of pain;
God will then restore them back to health.

4 'O Lord,' I prayed, 'Have mercy on me,
Heal me, for I've sinned against your laws.'

5 My enemies speak evil of me,
asking when I'll die and my name fade.

6 When they see me, they utter false words;
their hearts gather tales, and spread them far.

7 Whisp'ring, they spread their lies about me,
8 **'This illness is deadly. He'll not rise.'**

9 My trusted friend, who ate of my bread,
even he has turned against me now.

10 But you, O God, have mercy on me,
raise me up, then I shall pay them back.

12 In innocence, Lord, you sustained me
and let me gaze ever at your face.

Psalm 42

1 Like a deer, longs for water, my soul is thirsting for you.
**2 My soul thirsts for the living God,
when shall I come to him?**

3 Now my tears are my food, both by day and in the night hours,
**while all day long my foes are saying
'Where is your God now?'**

4 When I think of these things, I pour out my soul in sorrow:
how I led celebrating crowds into the house of God.

6 Why so heavy my soul, why so heavy in my spirit?
Yes why are you so wounded and so distressed within me?

7 Put your trust now in God, I will yet give him thanksgiving,
he is my saving presence, he's my helper and my God.

9 But now deep calls to deep in the thunder of your waters;
for all your waves and breakers they are sweeping over me.

10 Through the day's hours my God pours his endless love upon me.
At night his song is with me, it's a prayer to God, my life.

11 I say, 'Lord, you're my rock, why have I been so forgotten?
Why is my heart so heavy while my enemy attacks?'

14 Put your trust now in God, I will yet give him thanksgiving,
he is my saving presence, he's my helper and my God.

Psalm 43

1 Give me justice, O God, plead my cause against the godless;
O save me from deceitful lies and spiteful wicked souls.

2 You're my refuge O God; why then Lord did you reject me?
Why is my heart so heavy while my enemy attacks?

3 Send your light and your truth, send them so that they may lead me,
and bring me to your holy hill, your holy dwelling place.

4 That I may see God's altar, the God of joy and gladness;
and on the harp, give thanks to you,
give thanks to you my God.

5 Why so heavy my soul, why so heavy in my spirit?
O why are you so wounded and so distressed within me?

6 Put your trust now in God, I will yet give him thanksgiving,
he is my saving presence, he's my helper and my God.

Psalm 44

This psalm section *begins at verse 16.*

16 I am disgraced all the day long,
and my shame has now covered my whole face,

17 shamed at the sound of cursers taunts,
at the sight of the enemy's vengeance.

20 Yet we are crushed in jackals' haunts,
we are covered with darkness and shadow.

21 If we forget God's holy name,
or we stretch out our hands to a strange god,

22 will not our God search it all out?
For he knows all the secrets of our hearts.

23 But for your sake daily we're killed,
and are counted as sheep for the slaughter.

24 Rise up O Lord! Why do you sleep?
Awake Lord, do not leave us forever.

25 Why then, Lord, do you hide your face,
and forget all our grief and oppression?

26 Our soul is bowed down to the dust;
And our bodies lie flat on the cold earth.

27 Rise up, O Lord, rise to help us,
Come and ransom us for your dear love's sake.

Psalm 45

1 My heart is stirred with these most gracious words;
and to my King I give the songs I've made,
my tongue is like a ready writer's pen.

2 You are most handsome of all the men;
and graciousness, it rests upon your lips,
for God has blessed you now for evermore.

3 Strap your sword to your thigh, O mighty one;
put on your majesty and your glory.

4 Ride on and prosper in the cause of truth,
for righteousness and for humility.

6 Your throne, O God, shall last forever more.
The sceptre of your realm is righteousness.

7 You love true goodness, and you hate all crimes;
and God anoints you now above other kings.

8 You smell of aloes, myrrh, and cassia;
From iv-ory rooms the music brings you joy.

10 Daughters of kings are those in your favour.
At your right hand the queen is dressed in gold.

12 The people of Ty-re shall bring you gifts;
the richest ones seek favours from your throne.

17 'I'll make your name remembered evermore.
And peoples shall praise you from age to age.'

Psalm 46

1 God is our strength, our refuge here,
a present help in time of trouble;

2 we will not fear, though earth be moved,
though mountains tremble in the sea's heart;

3 though waters rage and waters foam,
though mountains quake before their surging.

4 A river makes God's city glad,
the holy place, where the Most High lives.

5 God is with her; she will not fall;
God shall help her as the new day dawns.

6 The nations roar, the kingdoms shake,
God speaks his word and then the earth melts.

8 Come look at all the works of God,
at this destruction he makes on earth.

9 He makes wars cease in all the world;
bows shattered, spears snapped, chariots burning.

10 'Be still, and know that I am God;
I will be lifted up in nations;
I will be lifted up on the earth.'

11 The Lord of hosts is with us now;
the God of Jacob is our stronghold.

Psalm 47

1 All you peoples, clap your hands together;
O sing to God with shouts of joy.

2 For the Lord Most High is to be fe-ared;
he is the great King over earth.

3 He subdued all the people beneath us
and all nations under our feet.

4 He has chosen our heritage for us,
in Jacob's pride, those whom he loves.

5 God has gone up with shouts of rejoicing,
the Lord with a great trumpet sound.

6 O sing praises to God, sing your praises;
sing praise to our King, sing your praise.

7 God is King, he's the king of the whole earth;
sing praises with all of your skill.

8 God reigns over each one of the nations;
God sits down on his holy throne.

9 All the rulers of nations are gathered,
the people of Abraham's God.

10 For the po-wers of earth are in God's hands
and he is raised up to the heights.

Psalm 48

1 Great is the Lord and highly to be praised,
in the city of our God.

2 His holy hill is fair and lifted high,
it's the joy of all the earth.

3 On Zi-on's mount, God's holy dwelling place,
stands the city of the king.

4 In these great halls our God has shown himself;
he will be a refuge place.

5 For now behold, earths kings are gathered here
and swept forward in their ranks.

6 They saw, and were astounded by the sight;
they fled in fear and dismay.

7 Great fear and trembling, terror seized them there;
agony like labour pains,

you smashed them like wrecked ships of Tarshish;
they were shattered by the wind.

8 As heard, we see, within God's great city,
God will make her truly safe.

9 We wait upon your loving kindness Lord,
wait within your temple's midst.

10 As with your name, with justice in your hand,
your praise reaches the earth's ends.

Psalm 49

1 O listen to me, all you people,
hear my words, all you who dwell in the world.

2 You people of high or low status,
rich ones and needy ones altogether.

3 My mouth shall speak words of great wisdom,
my heart shall speak from its understanding.

5 Why should I fear in times of evil,
when all my enemies' hate surrounds me?

7 For no-one can ransom a friend's life
or pay to God their deliverance price.

8 To ransom a soul is too costly;
the price is too high for any to pay,

9 For no-one can buy life unending,
or pay so others might not see the grave.

12 The honoured who lack understanding,
they'll perish, they're like the beasts who are doomed.

13 For this is the end of the boastful,
those ones who show delight in their own words.

17 Do not be afraid if some grow rich,
their households build up their honour and fame,

18 for they will keep nothing when they die,
nor will their fame follow when they are dead.

Psalm 50

1 The Lord, the mighty God has now spoken
and called the world to life from sunrise to dusk.

2 In beauty, out of Zi-on, God's light shines;
our Lord is coming and his voice won't be hushed.

4 He calls to earth, and calls to the hea-vens
to witness the almighty judgement of all.

5 Now gather all my faithful before me
who sealed my covenant with their sacrifice.

9 I do not need the bulls from your shelters,
nor the male goats you gave me out of your herds.

10 For the beasts of the forest are all mine,
mine are the cattle kept on thousands of hills.

11 I know each bird that flies on the mountains;
I own each creature, all that moves in the field.

13 Do you think that I eat from your fat bulls?
Do you think that I drink the blood of your goats?

14 Make thankfulness your sacrifice to him
and fulfil all the vows that you made to God.

15 Now call on me when you are in trouble;
for I will save you, and you will honour me.

Psalm 51

1 Have mercy on me, God in your goodness,
in your compassion blot out my stains.

2 O wash me tho-rough-ly from my evil
and cleanse me from all my deepest sin.

3 For I accept my faults and my failings
my sin is ever before my face.

4 Against you and you only have I sinned
and I've done evil within your sight.

5 So you are justified in your sentence;
you're truthful and you're a blameless judge.

8 Cleanse me with hyssop and I shall be clean;
wash me, and I'll be whiter than snow.

11 Create in me a clean heart, O Lord God,
re-gen-er-ate my spirit in me.

12 Do not cast me away from your presence,
don't take your Holy Spi-rit from me.

13 Give me again the joy of salvation;
grant me a willing spirit within;

14 then I shall teach your ways to the wicked
and sinners shall return back to you.

Psalm 52

1 Why boast in your evil, you tyrant,
when the goodness of God lasts forever?

2 Throughout the day you plot destruction,
and your tongue cuts the air like a razor.

3 You're expert at lying and falsehood,
and you love your lies more than sin-cer-ity.

4 You love to destroy with your cru'el words
and your tongue is a tongue of deception.

5 But at the last God will destroy you;
he'll snatch you from the tents of the living.

6 The just ones will see this and tremble;
they will laugh you to scorn and then they'll say:

7 'This one did not make God his stronghold,
but he trusted in riches and evil.'

8 I'm like a green tree in my God's house;
I will trust in God's goodness for ever.

9 I'll always thank you for what you've done;
I will hope in your name with the faithful.

Psalm 53

1 The fool speaks to himself, saying, 'There is no God.'
They're corrupt, their actions evil; no-one does any good.

2 God has looked down from Heav'n on the children of earth,
he'll see if any are wise enough to seek after God.

3 All have left the right path, they are all now corrupt;
there is no-one who does good now, there is not even one.

4 Will evil people learn, will they yet understand?
For like bread they chew my people, never calling on God?

5 They shall tremble with fear, fear they've not known before;
God will scatter all the bones of your besiegers at last.

6 You'll put them all to shame, they have been cast away.
7 O that Is-ra-el's salvation would now come out of Zion!

When our lives are restored then Is-rael shall rejoice,
and when God restores our fortunes Jacob too shall be glad.

Psalm 54.

1 Save me, O God, by your name;
defend me with your great po-wer.

2 Listen to my prayers, O Lord.
Listen to these words in my mouth.

3 Strangers are attacking me,
ruthless people they seek my life;
they do not know God or serve him.

4 Look, my God will be my help;
this is my God who supports me.

5 Evil rebounds on my foes;
you destroy them, you are faithful.

6 My heart's offe-ring I give you.
I praise your name for it is good.

7 For God saved me from my woes,
my eyes shall see my foes' downfall.

Psalm 55

1 Please hear my prayer, O Lord my God;
don't hide yourself from my petition.

2 Attend to me and answer me;
in my complaining I am distressed.

3 These hostile voices frighten me,
the wicked threaten and harass me;

4 They would bring evil down on me;
they're set against me in their fury.

5 My heart is anguished within me,
terrors of death have fallen on me.

6 Much fear and trembling has seized me,
horrible dread has overwhelmed me.

7 'O if I had the white dove's wings,
then I would fly off and be at rest.

8 For then I would fly far away
and make my home within the desert;

9 and I would make haste to escape
from raging winds and from the tempest.'

10 Confuse them Lord, divide their tongues,
for I have seen strife in the city.

Psalm 56.

1 Have mercy O God, for they trample on me;
they assault and oppress all day long.

2 My enemies trample me all the day long;
they are many who wage war on me.

3 In my day of fear I will put trust in you,
in my God whose good word I will praise.

4 My God I will praise, I will trust and not fear,
and so what can mere flesh do to me?

5 Yet all the day long my foes wound me with words;
for they think and they plot against me.

6 For they stir up trouble and they lie in wait;
they are tracking me, seeking my life.

7 But shall they escape from all their wicked deeds?
In your anger God, cast them all down.

8 You counted my groaning and bottled my tears;
and you wrote every one in your book.

9 My enemies turn, on the day I call you;
for I know that God is on my side.

10 My God I will praise, I will trust and not fear;
and so what can mere flesh do to me?

Psalm 57

1 Have mercy on me, have mercy my God,
for my soul it takes refuge in you;

2 I hide in the shade of your wondrous wings;
Hide until the disaster has passed.

3 I cry out to God, to God the Most High,
God will carry out his plans for me.

4 He will send his help from heav'n and save me
while rebuking those who oppress me;
God will send forth his faithful true love.

5 I lie in the midst of people like lions,
teeth like arrows, their tongues cut like swords.

6 Be lifted, O God, above all the hea-vens,
may your glory shine over the earth.

7 My foes dig their traps, I'm tir'd and dis-tressed
they dig pits and will fall in themselves.

8 My heart's ready Lord, my heart is prepared;
I will sing and make music of praise.

9 Awake, O my soul; awake, harp and lyre,
So that I may awaken the dawn.

10 I will thank you Lord, among all the realms;
With the peoples I will sing your praise.

Psalm 58

1 Do you speak out for justice, you powerful?
And do you give fair judgement to people?

2 No, you still plot injustice in your hearts;
and you spread vi-o-lence through the whole land.

3 From their wombs are the wicked perverted;
they are wicked from birth and speak foul lies.

4 They spit venom, it's vile like an adder;
they are like vipers, deaf, with their blocked ears.

5 in case they heed the voice of the charmer,
snakes ignoring the skilful spell-maker.

6 Smash the fangs in their poisoned mouths my Lord!
Tear the teeth from these li-ons O Lord God.

7 Let them vanish like water that drains off;
let them wither like grass crushed beneath feet.

9 Lest they stretch out their thorns like a bramble,
thorns, both green and dry, sweep them away Lord,

10 All the just rejoice see-ing God's vengeance;
11 Truly God will judge and harvest this earth.

Psalm 59.

1 Come rescue me from my enemies Lord;
set me high above those who rise against me.

2 Save me from all those who do evil deeds;
come rescue me from all these murderous ones.

3 See how my foes lie in wait for my soul;
they stir up their trouble through no fault of mine.

4 Awaken Lord, give me help, and you'll see;
for you are the God of the armies of heav'n.

7 They come at nightfall and then snarl like dogs,
they prowl through the streets of the city at night.

8 They pour out such evil words with their mouths;
'So who then is go-ing to hear us?' they sneer.

9 But you, O Lord, you will laugh them to scorn;
you hold all those nations and give them disdain.

11 My God, in his love, he will come to me;
he'll show me the downfall of all of my foes.

18 But as for me, I will sing of your strength;
each morning I will praise your love and your care.

19 You are my stronghold of unfailing love.
20 **You will be my refuge when trouble hits me.**

Psalm 60

1 O my God, you've rejected and broken us;
you were angry, restore us again.

2 You have shaken the earth, it is torn apart;
heal the earth's wounds, it trembles and shakes.

3 You have made these your people drink bitter things;
and we sway from the wine you gave us.

4 You have raised up a sign for your followers
so we flee from the face of the bow

5 Give salvation with your right-hand, hear our cries,
that the people you love may be saved.

7 Gi-le-ad is mine, and Ma-na-sseh is mine;
E-phra-im my helm, Judah my staff.

8 Mo-ab my washpot, on E-dom I cast shoes;
on Phil-is-tia I tri-umph and shout.

9 Who will take me to your fortified city?
Who will bring me out into E-dom?

10 Have you now, O my Lord God, rejected us?
Will you no longer walk with our troops?

11 Grant us help, for we humans can't help ourselves
12 **With the Lord's help we will do great acts.**

Psalm 61.

1 O hear my crying, O God,
and listen now to my prayer.

2 From the earth's end I call to you with fainting heart;
O lead me to the rock that is higher than I.

3 For you're my refuge and strength,
a tow'r of strength against foes.

4 Let me live in your tent and linger ever more.
And take refuge in safety beneath your wings' shade.

5 For you, O God, hear my vows;
our riches fearing your name.

6 You will add length of days to the life of the king,
that his years may endure through all gen-er-a-tions.

7 May he sit throned evermore;
may love keep watch over him.

8 So will I always sing to the praise of your name,
and so day after day will fulfil all my vows.

Psalm 62

1 My soul in stillness waits, it waits for God alone;
from God alone will come my salvation.

2 God only is my rock, my rock and saving help,
my stronghold, so I shall not be shaken.

3 How long will you attack and try to destroy me,
like leaning walls or unstable fences?

5 Wait on God O my soul, in stillness wait for him;
my hope is in my God, who is my rock.

7 God is my might and strength, my glory is in God.
God is my strong rock, he is my shelter.

8 O put your trust in God, my people trust in him;
Pour out your hearts before God, our refuge.

9 The peoples are just breath, they are an illusion;
when weighed these people are lighter than air.

10 Take no pride in your theft, don't trust those who oppress;
though fortunes grow, don't set your heart on them.

11 For God spoke the word once, and twice I heard the same,
the power belongs to God and God only.

12 True steadfast love is yours, belonging to you Lord,
you will reward the people for their deeds.

Psalm 63

1 O God, you are my God, I seek you eagerly;
my soul is thirsting for you, the true living God.

2 O God, you are my God, my body pines for you
in dry and thirsty lands where no fresh water runs.

3 I've come before you now, into your holy place,
so that I might see all of your glory and pow'r.

4 Far better than my life is your love and your grace
5 and I will praise your name for as long as I live.

I will lift up my hands and praise your holy name.
6 My soul shall be content with the ripest fruit trees.

7 For when I lie awake, recalling you in bed,
I meditate upon you throughout the night watch.

8 For you have always been my helper and my help
and under your wings' shadow I can now rejoice.

9 My soul it clings to you, your right hand holds me fast
10 but those who seek my soul shall sink into the earth.

11 Let them fall by their sword becoming food for dogs.
12 The king shall praise the Lord, and his people be glad.

Psalm 64

1 Hear me O my God, the voice of my complaint;
and preserve my life from my enemies' threats.

2 Now hide me from all the wicked gath-er-ings,
from wrongdoers and those who wish me evil.

3 They sharpen their tongues like they sharpen a sword;
they aim bitter words like they aim an arrow.

4 So that they may shoot the blameless from their dens;
suddenly they shoot and then they are not seen.

5 For they will hold fast to all their evil ways;
they talk of their snares saying 'Who will see us?'

6 They seek wickedness and lay a cunning trap,
For the minds and hearts of the people are deep.

7 Swiftly God himself will shoot them with his darts,
suddenly they shall then be wounded themselves.

8 The words of their tongues shall be their own downfall,
all who see them shake their heads in derision.

9 People shall then fear, proclaiming all God's deeds,
they'll tell of God's works, they shall have joy in him.

10 They shall put their trust within the Lord their God.
All the true of heart glorify the Lord God.

Psalm 65

1 Praise is due to you, O God, in Zi-on;
we shall pay our vows to you who answer prayer.

2 When our evil seems to overwhelm us
you forgive our sins, you wipe them all away.

5 Your strength circles mountains with your power.
6 You silence the seas and raging of the crowds.

7 Earth's ends dwellers tremble at your marvels;
gates of morning and of evening sing your praise.

8 Visiting the earth you bless it with rain;
9 you make grain for all and you provide for earth.

10 You drench furrows, you smooth out the ridges;
you soften the ground with rain, and bless its growth.

11 O Lord, with your goodness you crown the year,
and your pathways overflow with fruitfulness.

12 May the wilderness grow green with goodness;
may the hills around them be encased in joy.

13 May the meadows be clothed with flocks of sheep;
valleys stand so thick with corn that they will sing.

Psalm 66

1 O be joyful in God, all the earth;
hymn his glory and sing to his name;
shout out loud, give him glo-ri-ous praise.

2 Say to God, 'Awesome are all your deeds!
Your strength makes all your enemies quake'.

4 Come and see the great works of your God,
how his dealings are wondrous with all.

6 In his might he eternally rules;
his eyes keep watch on all nation states;
let the rebels not rise against him.

7 Bless our God, you, his peoples, praise him;
make the voice of his praise to be heard,

8 Praise the God who gave life to our souls;
who will not let our feet slip or fall.

14 Come and listen, all you who fear God,
I will tell what he did for my soul.

15 When I cried out to him with my mouth
his praise was always there on my tongue.

16 If I had nourished evil within,
then the Lord would not listen to me.

17 But in truth God has surely heard me;
he has heard the poor voice of my prayer.

Psalm 67

1 Lord God have mercy, come and bless us
and make your face shine with favour on us.

2 May all your ways be known on the earth,
your saving pow'r in all nations of earth.

3 Let all the peoples praise you,O God;
let people, all people praise you O God.

4 Let nations all be glad and rejoice,
you judge all justly and govern the earth.

5 Let all the peoples praise you,O God;
let people, all people praise you O God.

6 Then shall the earth bring forth all her fruits,
and God, our own God, will richly bless us.

7 Pour out your blessing, come and bless us
and all the ends of the earth shall fear him.

Psalm 68

1 Let God arise and let his enemies be scattered;
and let those who hate him flee before his face.

2 As rising smoke dissolves so then they will all vanish,
as wax melts in fi-re, so the wicked die.

3 But let the righteous sing to God with loud rejoicing;
pave the way for our Lord, who rides on the clouds.

5 Father of fatherless, defender of the widows,
such is God within his holy dwelling place.

6 God houses homeless and gives welcome to the priso-ners,
but the rebels live in burning sun-scorched lands.

17 You have gone up on high, you took the jailers captive;
you have received tribute, even from your foes.

20 Then God will smash the heads of all foes and attackers,
hairy scalps of those who walk in wicked ways.

27 Call forth your might O God, and show your mighty po-wer;
show your strength O God as you have done before.

28 For your sake kings will bring their gifts in Je-ru-sa-lem.
30 Scatter all the peoples who delight in war.

32 Sing to God, kingdoms of the earth, come hymn your master;
make exquisite music to the praise of God.

Psalm 69

1 Please save me, O God, for the waters reach my neck.
2 I swim in the swamp where there is no foothold.

I come to deep waters and their flood swallows me.
3 I'm weary with crying; my throat skinned and raw;

Now my eyes are failing from searching for my God.
10 I love your Great House, scorning you insults me.

11/12 I fasted in sackcloth, they turned and taunted me.
22 Their taunts broke my heart; I am filled with sadness.

22 I looked for some comfort, but no-one pitied me.
23 They gave gall to eat, vinegar for my drink.

28 They persecute the one that you have stricken down,
and increase the sorrows of him that you pierced.

24 Make their meals a trap, and their sacred feasts a snare.
30 Blot them from your book, don't list them as righteous.

32 I praise God in song, and proclaim in gratitude.
34 The humble are glad, seek God, and your heart lives.

37 For God will save Zi-on and rebuild Judah's towns
38 and God's loving children, they will live in them.

Psalm 70

1 O God, make speed to save me;
O Lord, make haste to help me.

2 Let those who want to kill me
be shamed and sent confusion;

now turn them back in their shame;
all those who jeer and mock me.

3 Let those who mock and taunt me
be turned back in their shaming.

4 Let there be joy and gladness
for all who seek your face Lord.

Let those who love your po-wer
Say 'God is great.' forever.

5 But me, I'm poor and needy;
come Lord, and help me quickly.

6 You are my help, my saviour;
O Lord, do not delay now.

Psalm 71

1 I have taken shelter in you my Lord;
let me not be put to shame.

2 Save me, set me free in your righteousness;
turn your ear to me, save me!

3 Be a mighty fortress where I can come;
send help, save me, my stronghold.

4 Save me, O my God, from all wicked hands,
from the grasp of autocrats.

5 For you have been my hope, O Sovereign God,
confidence, even from youth.

6 I've depended on you even from birth,
you drew me out from the womb;
and I will always praise you.

7 I've become a sign to many on earth,
but you are my strong refuge.

8 Let my mouth be ever full of your praise
and your glory all day long.

9 Don't cast me away when I reach old age;
don't leave me when my strength fails.

12 Lord be not far from me, help me, my God.
21 Raise my honour, comfort me.

Psalm 72

1 Give the king your judgements O my God,
and your justice to the Kings Son.

8 May his rule stretch out from sea to sea;
from the river to the earth's end.

9 May his foes all kneel before his throne;
enemies of his will lick dust.

10 Kings of Tarshish and the isles shall bow;
Sheba's kings and Seba's bring gifts.

11 Rulers of Earth, fall down at His feet;
eve-ry nation give him service.

12 Ran-som-ing all those who cry for help.
Those who have no earthly helper.

13 He shall save the weak and save the poor;
save the lives of all the needy.

14 From oppression he redeems their souls,
and their blood is precious to him.

15 Long may he live, may he gather gold.
Gold from Sheba, poured at his feet;

and prayer sent to hea-ven without end.
May they bless him all the day long.

Psalm 73

1 Truly, God is good to Is-ra-el,
good to all those who are pure in heart.

2 But for me; my feet had almost slipped
and then I nearly lost my foothold.

3 For I envied those arrogant ones;
when I witnessed the prosperous bad;

4 For they suffer no pains or distress
and their bodies are healthy and strong.

5 They have no troubles, no mis-for-tunes;
nor are they plagued like ord-in-ary folk;

6 Therefore pride is their necklace with jew'ls
and their vio-lence wraps them like a cloak.

7 Their iniquity comes from within;
the conceit in their hearts overflows.

17 Till I went in the sanct-uary of God
and I grasped what their ending would be:

18 You've put them on a sli-pper-y path;
you slide them to their own de-struc-tion.

19 In an instant then they are destroyed,
and they perish, in fear at the end.

Psalm 74

1 O God, why have you rejected your tribes?
And why does your anger blaze at your own sheep?

2 Remember your flock you bought from of old,
the tribe you have purchased, Mount Zion where you live.

3 O hasten your steps to these endless ruins,
where enemies laid waste your most holy place.

11 Yet God is my king, my king from of old,
who saved us with deeds in the depths of the earth.

12 It's you, Lord, who cleaved the sea with your might
and shattered the dragons'-heads on the sea-foam.

15 For yours is the day, and yours is the night;
and you have created the moon and the sun.

19 In pity, O Lord, gaze on our poor world.
We're haunted with vio-lence, the earth is so dark.

20 Don't let the oppressed be shamed and cast-out;
let poor ones and needy ones praise your great name.

21 Arise O my Lord and uphold your cause;
remember how senseless ones scoff all day long

22 and never forget the noise of your foes,
the unending uproar of those who cross you.

Psalm 75

1 We give you thanks, O God, we give you thanks,
for your name Lord is near, your deeds declare.

2 The Lord says 'When I choose th'ap-poin-ted time;
I will judge all the earth with honesty.'

3 Though the earth shakes and all its people quake,
I will hold up her pillars, strong and firm.

4 I warned the proud 'Stop all your boasting now,'
I warned the wicked 'Do not flaunt your strength.

5 Do not raise up your horns and flaunt your strength;
do not speak arrogantly or with pride.'

6 O not from the east, neither from the west,
nor from the wilderness comes fame and power.

7 But God alone, the Lord will be the judge;
he casts one person down to raise one up.

8 For in the hand of God there is a cup,
a cup well-spiced of full and foaming wine.

9 He pours it for the wicked of the earth;
he pours it out, they drain it to the dregs.

10 But as for me, for ever I'll rejoice,
I will make music to the Lord our God.

11 The po-wer of the wicked I will break;
the po-wer of the righteous souls will grow.

Psalm 76

1 Our God is known in Judah;
his name is great in Is-ra-el.

2 Je-ru-sa-lem his temple,
Mount Zi-on is His dwelling place.

3 He broke the fiery arrows,
the shield, the sword, and war's weapons.

4 You come with light of splendour,
far mightier than the wild mountains.

5 The sleeping knights were plundered,
none of the war-riors can strike back.

6 At your roar, God of Jacob,
both horse and cha-riot fell down stunned.

7 Your Majesty strikes terror:
who stands before your angry face?

10 You crushed the people's anger,
your wrath's survivors bound in chains.

11 Make vows to God, fulfil them;
**let all around him bring their gifts
to God, most worthy to be feared.**

12 He breaks down all earth's princes;
strikes terror in the hearts of kings.

Psalm 77

1 I cry out to my God, cry for help;
I cry loudly, I know God will hear me.

2 In my day of distress I sought God;
in the night I refuse consolation.

3 Now I think upon God and I groan;
as I ponder, my spirit is fainting.

4 For you will not let my eyelids close;
I am so troubled I have gone silent.

5 I consider the great days of old;
I remember the years that have long gone;

6 I commune with my heart in the night;
and my spirit it searches for meaning.

7 Will the Lord cast us off evermore?
Will he never again look with favour?

8 Has his kindness gone for ever more?
Has his promise now ended forever?

10 Then I thought, 'To this I will appeal:
I'll remember the deeds of the Most High.

11 I'll remember the works of the Lord;
I'll remember the wonders of old time.'

Psalm 78a

1 Come hear my teaching O my people;
incline your ears to the words of my mouth.

2 In parables I will declare it;
I'll pour forth mysteries from times of old,

3 such things as we have heard and then known,
which all our ancestors, they have told us.

4 We will not hide this from their children,
but will recount for the people to come,

the glor-ious deeds of God Almighty,
and all the wonderful works he has done.

5 He gave the law, he ordered Is-rael,
and he commanded them to teach their young;

6 that children yet unborn might know this,
that they might tell it to those yet to come;

7 so that they might put their trust in God
and not forget the great deeds of our God,

but keep his laws and his commandments,
8 not like their ancestors, stubborn and false,

a treach-erous faithless ge-ne-ra-tion
who were not steadfast or faithful to God.

Psalm 78b

This psalm section begins at verse 9.

9 The children of Eph-ra-im, armed with the bow,
 they turned tail and ran and deserted the fight;

10 The cove-nant of God they transgressed and despised
and refused to follow and walk in his law;

12 yet he did great marvels in their forebears sight,
13 he parted the sea and he let them pass through.

17 Despite all these works they still sinned against him;
they defied the Most High in the wilderness

22 For they had no faith in their Lord and their God
and put no trust in him or his saving help.

23 And so he commanded and opened the clouds;
24 he rained on them manna, the grain of the heav'ns.

37 Their hearts were not faithful to him or his pact,
38 but he had such mercy he forgave their crimes.

39 He recalled that they were but flesh or a breath;
a short breeze that passes and does not return,

54 and he led them safely to his holy place,
the mountain which his mighty right hand had won.

55 He drove out the nations, shared out their estates;
he settled all Is-ra-el's tribes in their tents.

Psalm 79

1 O Lord God, evil nations have destroyed your heritage;
**they profaned your great temple, they destroyed
Je-ru-sa-lem.**

2 They left your servants' bodies as a food for flying birds,
fed the flesh of your faithful to the wild beasts of the field.

3 Their blood they shed like water all around Je-ru-sa-lem,
for they spared not a single soul to bury all the dead.

4 Mocked and taunted by neighbours, we are scorned by all around,
5 how long will you be angry and your fury blaze like fire?

6 Pour your rage on the nations that have never known your love,
and upon all the kingdoms who have not called on your name.

7 They de-voured all of Jacob, they laid-waste his dwelling place.
8 In compassion, forgive us Lord, we are brought very low.

9 Help us, God our salvation, for the glory of your name;
10 Why should heathens then taunt us saying,
 'Where is now their God?'

12 Hear the sighing of pris-oners, and preserve those doomed to die.
13 May the taunts of our neighbours, be paid-back sev'n times again.

14 And yet we are your people, and we are your pasture's sheep.
We will give thanks forever, through all ages give you praise.

Psalm 80

1 Listen, O Shepherd of all Israel,
you that led Joseph's people like a flock;

2 Shine forth, O God, enthroned on cherubim,
with Eph-ra-im, Ma-na-sseh, Ben-ja-min.

3 Stir up your strength, stir up your awesome strength.
Come Lord to save us, come and save us all!

4 Turn us again, O God, now turn us back;
show the light of your face, and we'll be saved.

5 Lord God of all the armies of the heav'ns,
how long will you rage at your people's prayer?

6 You feed them with the bread of their own tears;
you give full measures of their tears to drink.

7 We're subjects of our near-neighbours' distain.
Our enemies? They laugh us all to scorn!

8 Turn us again, O God of hea-ven's hosts;
show the light of your face, and we'll be saved.

9 You brought a vine from out of Egypt's land;
you drove out nations and you planted it.

10 You cleared the ground and then gave it some room,
when it had grown good roots, it filled the land.

Psalm 81

1 Sing merrily to God our strength,
hymn in joy the God of Jacob.

2 Take up the song and sound the drum,
play the harp and tuneful ly-re.

3 Blow trumpet calls at the new moon,
at full moon, our solemn feast day.

4 This is a law for Is-ra-el,
statutes of the God of Jacob.

5 The charge he laid on Joseph's tribes,
when they came from out of Egypt.

6 I heard a voice I did not know:
'I took burdens from their shoulders;
their hands were freed from their burdens.

7 You called on me and I saved you;
I responded from the thunder;
at Mer-i-bah you were tested.

8 Hear, O my people, I'll warn you:
Is-rael, if you'd only listen!

9 There will be no strange gods with you;
Never worship foreign idols.

10 I rescued you from Egypt's land;
I shall fill your mouth with good things.'

Psalm 82

1 Our God takes his stand in the council of hea-ven;
Among all the gods he will render his judgement:

2 How long will you cheat and then give unjust verdicts
How long will you favour the cause of the wicked?

3 Be fair to the weak and be fair to the orphan
and maintain the rights of the poor and the needy.

4 Come rescue the weak hands and rescue the needy;
Deliver them all from the hands of the wicked.

5 They do not have knowledge they do not have wisdom,
for they stumble still and they walk in the darkness.
The pillars of earth they are now being shaken.

6 Though you are called gods by me, the Most High's children
7 like humans you'll die and fall down like their princes.

8 Arise Elohim, O my God, judge the earth now,
For to you O God, belong all of the nations.

Psalm 83

1 Do not hold your peace Lord, don't be silent;
do not fail to be moved O my Lord.

2 For your enemies raise up a tumult,
and now those who hate you lift their heads.

3 They plot wickedness over your people
and they plot against your treasured ones.

4 They say 'Let us wipe out all this nation
that all kingdoms forget Israel's name.'

5 They have plotted together as one mind
and now they are in league against you.

13 May they leave like the seeds from the thistles.
Drive them out like the chaff in the wind.

14 Like the fire that burns up all the forest;
like the flame that sets mountains ablaze.

16 And then cover their faces with shame Lord
that they might seek your face and your name.

17 O let them be disgraced now forever
and let them be confused and then die.

18 Let them know you alone, are the Most High,
for you are Most High upon earth.

Psalm 84

1 How lovely is your house O God of Hea-ven's hosts,
my soul aches and longs for just a glimpse.

2 My heart and flesh cry out. The sparrow finds her home,
and the swallow nests before your throne.

3 How blest are they who live, who live within your house;
they will be forever praising you.

4 How blest are those who find their energy in you,
in whose heart are Zi-on's paths and roads;

5 who walking through the wastes can find a water-spring,
for the rains of autumn bless their routes.

9 For one day in your house, a day spent in your courts
is more than a thousand days elsewhere.

10 I'd rather stand and guard the threshold of your house
than spend time within the wicked tents.

11 God is both sun and shield, is glor-ious and grace-filled;
no good thing will he keep from the just.

12 O God of Hea-ven's armies O Lord God of hosts,
blest are those who put their trust in you.

Psalm 85

1 Lord you were gracious and kind to your land;
you restored Jacob and freed him from chains.

2 You forgave people their faults and their guilt;
you pardoned wrongs and you covered their sins.

4 Lord God our Saviour restore us again,
let all your anger now come to an end.

5 Will you be angry forever with us?
Will all your anger last from age to age?

6 Will you not bring us to life once again,
so that your people can have joy in you?

7 Show us your kindness and mercy O God,
grant us salvation, your rescue, your love.

9 Salvation is near for those who fear God,
God's glory shines, it will shine in our land.

10 Mercy and truth, came together and met,
justice and peace came together and kissed.

11 Truth, it shall spring from the depths of the earth;
right-eous-ness, it will look down from the heav'ns.

12 Our Lord God will give us all that is good,
and the good earth shall pour its produce out.

Psalm 86

1 Bend down your ear Lord, and answer me,
I am very poor and in misery.

2 Preserve my soul, I'm faithful to you;
save your servant for I do trust in you.

3 Have mercy on me Lord, you're my God;
I call out for you, I call all day long.

4 Gladden your servant, your servant's soul,
for to you O Lord, I lift up my soul.

6 Lord listen to the voice of my prayer;
listen to the sound of my anguished pleas.

7 In my distress I shall call on you,
and I know you'll answer, you'll answer me.

9 Nations you made will worship you Lord;
all the nations come and honour your name.

10 For you are great and do marve-llous things
you alone are great, you only are God.

11 Teach me your ways, I'll walk in your truth;
knit my heart to you, to honour your name.

17 Show me your favour, shame all my foes;
you have helped me and have com-for-ted me.

Psalm 87

1 Founded by God upon the holy mountains;
**God loves the gates of Zi-on
more than all of Jacob's homes.**

2 Glor-i-ous things of you are truly spoken,
O Glor-i-ous Je-ru-sa-lem, the city of our God.

3 Egypt and Babylon I count, they know me,
Phil-is-ti-a, Ty-re and Cush; in Zi-on they were born.

4 Of Zion they'll say, 'This one was born within her,
**the Most High has established her,
the most High God himself.'**

5 God will write down the register of peoples,
**'This one also was born there,
He was born within this place.'**

6 And as they dance, with music they'll be singing.
**'My wellsprings are in you my God.
My wellsprings are in you.'**

Psalm 88

1 O Lord my God, you are my saving God,
in your presence I cry all day and night.

2 Into your presence let all my prayers come;
Lord bend down your ear to hear my sad songs.

3 My soul is full, full of troubles and woes,
my life's drawing near to the land of death.

7 You've laid me down in the depths of the pit,
in a place of darkness in the abyss.

8 Your anger weighs down on me heavily,
and I drown beneath the power of your waves.

9 You've put my friends far away, far from me;
you have made me hateful, hateful to them.

10 I'm locked away and I cannot get free;
my eyes fail from all the trouble I am in.

15 But as for me Lord I will cry to you;
early in the morning I pray to you.

16 Lord why have you now rejected my soul?
Why have you now hidden your face from me?

20 My friends, my loved ones, you put far from me
and hid my companions out of my sight.

Psalm 89

1 My song shall always sing of the kindness of my God;
I'll proclaim your faithfulness through generations.

2 Your kindness, I declare, it will last forever more;
you have set your faithfulness as firm as hea-ven.

3 You said, 'I made a promise before my chosen one;
I have sworn an oath to King David my servant:

4 for your seed and your line I'll establish evermore
and build up your throne throughout all generations.'

5 Now the hea-vens shall praise all your wonders, O my God,
and your faithfulness within the great assembly.

8 Who is there like you Lord? Who is like you, God of hosts?
Mighty loving Lord, your faithfulness surrounds you.

9 It is you who can rule all the raging of the sea;
and you still the mighty waters when they rise up.

12 You made the Northern lands, you created all the South,
and Mount Tabor and Mount Herman have joy in you.

15 Joyful are all the people who know the triumph shout:
For they walk O God within the light of your face.

26 He shall call me, 'My father, the rock of my rescue:'
27 I will make him my firstborn high over all kings.

Psalm 90

1 Lord you've been our refuge, our safe place,
from one generation to the next.

2 Before all the mountains were brought forth
or all of this world was ever formed,

you are God from everlasting days.
Eternal, forever, you are God.

3 Lord you turn us back to dust and say;
'Turn back, all you children of the Earth.'

4 For one thousand years are as one day,
that passes as shifts within the night.

10 Our life can span years, three score and ten,
 or if our strength lasts, perhaps four score;

yet all of their sum is pain and toil.
12 Teach us to count all our days aright

that we may gain wisdom in our hearts.
For our days will pass and we'll be gone.

13 Turn back Lord again, why this delay?
14 Show your morning kindness, bring us joy.

17 May God's gracious favour rest on us
and prosper the work of all our hands.

Psalm 91

1 Those who dwell, shel-te-ring by the Most High;
those who live in the shadow of God,

2 'You're my refuge, my fort' they'll say to God,
'my God, in you I will put my trust.'

3 He shall save you from snares and from hunters,
save you all from the terr-i-ble plague.

4 He will cover you, safe in his feathers;
faith and truth, they will then be your shield.

5 You shall not fear the terrors of night-time,
nor the arrows that fly in the day,

6 You'll not fear the plague stalking in darkness,
nor the sickness that rages at noon,

7 And though thousands fall by you, ten thousand,
though they fall it shall never reach you.

11 He shall order his angels to keep you,
they will guard you in all of your ways.

12 They shall keep you, hold you safe in their hands.
You will not bruise your foot on a stone.

15 They will call on me and I will answer;
I will save them, and I'll honour them.

Psalm 92

1 O it is a good thing to give thanks to God;
to sing and make praise to your name O Most High.

2 To tell of your love as the morning first dawns,
and speak of your faithfulness during the night.

3 On great ten-stringed instruments and on the harp,
and sing to the melody of the sweet lyre.

4 You made me rejoice, O my Lord, by your acts,
I sing in my joy at the work of your hands.

5 How great are your works, Lord, your thoughts are so deep.
6 The senseless don't know this or fools understand;

7 Though wicked and evil ones flourish like grass
8 they will be destroyed, but you Lord are raised up.

12 The good are like palm trees, like cedars they spread;
14 they bear fruit in old age, they're vig-orous and green.

Psalm 93

1 The Lord our God is king and he has dressed himself in glory;
he wraps himself in glory circled in a belt of strength.

2 He made the whole world sure and firm so it cannot be shaken.
3 Your throne stands firm and true from old;
an everlasting God.

4 The floods have lifted up, O Lord, have lifted up their voices;
the floods lift up their voice O Lord, the waves lift up their roar.

5 Far migh-tier than the water's thunder, migh-tier than the breakers,
Our mighty and majestic God is migh-tier than them all.

6 Your testimonies, they are sure; your statutes they are faithful,
and holiness adorns your house, O Lord for ever more.

Psalm 94

1 Lord God, avenging God shine forth,
2 rise up O Lord and judge the earth.

4 How long will evildoers boast
and pour out proud and wicked words?

5 They crush your people down O Lord,
and trouble your inheritance.

6 Strangers and widows they oppress;
and put the fatherless to death.

16 Who'll rise against the evil ones?
Defend us from the wicked hearts?

17 If God had never helped my cause,
I would be silent in the pit.

18 And when I said 'My foot has slipped,'
your loving mercy helped me up.

19 When many worries filled my heart,
your care revived my thirsty soul.

22 God is my castle and my keep;
the mighty rock in which I trust;

23 silencing wicked, cruel plans,
turning their evil back on them.

Psalm 95

1 O come now! Let us sing to the Lord;
in the rock of salvation rejoice.

2 Let us come to his presence with thanks;
make a joyful noise with songs of praise.

3 For the Lord is Almighty and God
and a great King above other gods.

4 He holds all the deep places of earth
and he holds all the strength of the hills.

5 He filled up all the pools of the sea;
like a sculptor he carved earth and land.

6 Let us come now and bow, bend our knees
come, and facing our Maker, kneel down.

7 For he is our Lord and he's our God
and we are like the sheep in his hands.

8 Listen out for his voice, listen out:
Do not harden your hearts as before

9 when your ancestors asked me for proof
even though they had seen acts of power.

10 Forty years I detested those tribes
for these people are far from my ways.

Psalm 96

1 Sing to the Lord, O sing a new song;
sing to the Lord, sing all the earth.

2 Sing to the Lord and praise his great name;
Spread the good news of his release.

3 Tell nations of his glory and fame;
his wonders tell to all the lands.

4 Great is our God, and mightily praised;
awesome is he beyond all gods.

5 Those people's Gods are idols, no more ;
our God has made hea-ven and earth.

6 Greatness and honour go before him;
splendour within his holy place.

9 Worship in beauty and holiness;
tremble before him all the earth.

10 'Our God is king,' let all nations know.
He made earth firm, it can't be moved;
he will judge all with right-eous-ness.

12 Let fields be glad and filled with delight;
trees of the wood, shout out for joy.

13 Rejoice creation, God's coming soon,
coming in truth to judge the earth.

Psalm 97

1 The Lord God is king: earth rejoice now;
let all of the islands be glad.

2 Thick darkness and clouds they surround him;
With justice the base of his throne.

3 Before him there goes burning fi-re
to burn up all his enemies.

4 His lightnings they light up the whole world;
the earth looked upon it and shook.

5 The mountains will melt at God's presence,
on seeing the Lord of all Earth.

6 The hea-vens proclaim his perfection,
his glory all peoples have seen.

7 But those who serve idols will be shamed.
Bow down at his feet worthless gods.

8 Then Zi-on rejoiced, Judah was glad,
because of your judgements, O Lord.

9 You are the Most High over all earth;
exalted far over all gods.

11 A light has sprung up for the righteous,
and great joy for those true in heart.

Psalm 98

1 O sing to the Lord, sing a new song,
for he has done mar-ve-llous things.

2 His own right hand has won the vic-tory,
his right hand and his holy arm.

3 The Lord has made known his salvation;
de-live-rance the nations have seen.

4 He remembers his love of Is-rael;
salvation the earth's ends have seen.

5 Sing praises to God, sing out all earth;
burst forth into singing and hymns.

6 Make music to God with the harp strings,
with melody, harp, lyre and song.

7 With trumpets and sound of the ram's horn
shout praises before God your king.

8 Let everything in the sea thunder,
the world and those dwelling within.

9 Let mountains together sing gladly;
let rivers and streams clap their hands,

10 for our God is coming in judgement,
in fairness, and justice, and truth.

Psalm 99

1 The Lord is our king: let the peoples tremble;
throned above the cherubim: then let the earth shake.

2 The Lord is exalted and great in Zi-on;
high above all peoples, God is great in Zi-on.

3 Let them praise your name, which is great and awesome;
let them praise your name, the Lord our God is holy.

4 Our Almighty King, you've established justice;
in your land of Jacob you have been just and right.

5 Now lift up the Lord, bow before his footstool;
bow down at his footstool, for the Lord is holy.

6 God's priests; Moses, Aaron and Sam-uel called out;
he answered them when they called upon the Lord God.

7 He spoke to them out of a pillar of cloud;
they kept all his statutes and the law he gave them.

8 You answered your servants; O Lord our great God;
you forgave the Israelites. You pardoned their wrongs.

9 Now lift up the Lord, bow before his mountain;
worship on his holy hill, the Lord is holy.

Psalm 100

1 Rejoice in your God all you lands,
and serve God with gladness, come singing for joy.

2 Now know that the Lord is your God;
it is he who made us and we are now his;

now know that the Lord is your God,
and we are his people, the sheep of his flock.

3 Come into his gates giving thanks;
now enter his courts with your praise and your song.

Come now, celebrate, bless his name,
4 for our God is gracious; his love never ends.

Come now, celebrate , bless his name,
through each generation his faithfulness lasts.

Psalm 101

1 I will sing of your kindness and justice;
to you, my God, I will sing.

2 Make me wise in the way of the blameless:
O when will you come to me?

3 I will walk with a vir-tu-ous pure heart
within the walls of my house.

4 I'll not place in the gaze of my eyesight
Some base or wicked id-ea.

5 I hate evil; and devious actions;
they shall not cling to my soul.

7 Those who slander their neighbour in secret
I'll silence with utmost speed.

8 Those with proud eyes and arrogant natures
I will not welcome with me.

10 Those who walk in the way that is blameless,
my servants these ones shall be.

11 Wicked, wrong-do-ers and the deceitful,
these shall not dwell in my house.

12 Those who lie and the tellers of falsehoods,
these shall not live in my sight.

Psalm 102

1 O Lord, hear my prayer, let my crying come to you.
2 Do not hide your face in the day of my distress.

3 O bend down your ear, turn your ear and hear my cry;
the day that I call, Lord please answer speedily.

4 My days disappear as the embers from the fire;
my bones burn like embers within a furnace flame.

5 My heart it is broken and withered like the grass;
10 I've mingled my drinking cup with my salty tears.

13 But you O my Lord are enthroned forever more,
through all generations your holy name will last.

14 For you will rise up, and take pity upon Zion;
It's time for some mercy, the scheduled time has come.

26 As time dawned you formed all the bedrock of the earth,
the hea-vens above are your fingers' handiwork;

27 the hea-vens shall perish, but your love shall endure;
whilst they will wear out like a garment that is torn.

28 You'll change them like clothing, and then they shall be changed;
you're ever the same, and your years will never fail.

29 The heirs of your servants dwell safely ever more,
for their progeny are established in your sight.

Psalm 103

1 Bless the Lord, bless the Lord O my soul,
and all that is in me bless his name.

2 Bless the Lord, bless the Lord O my soul,
his blessings you never should forget;

4 God who brings you up from the dark Pit;
you're crowned with compassion and with love;

5 your life is satisfied with good things,
like eagles your youth is then renewed.

6 God's ways are righteous and they are true
with justice for all who are oppressed.

7 He made known to Moses all his ways;
his works to the youth of Is-ra-el.

8 God is compassionate, merciful,
 yet patient in rage, a fount of love.

11 High as hea-ven is high over earth,
so strong is his love for the devout.

12 Far as east is removed from the west,
this far has he sent away our sins.

14 For God knows of what things we are made;
he knows and remembers we are dust.

Psalm 104

1 Now bless the Lord God, O my heartstrings.
My God, you are great and majestic!

4 You use the white clouds as your cha-riot;
you ride on the wings of the breezes.

14 You water the hills from your dwelling;
you fill up the earth with your artworks.

15 You cause grass to grow for the cattle
and green plants to meet our requirements,

16 they grow from the earth bringing good food
and good wine to gladden our heartstrings.

26 O Lord God how many are your works!
In wisdom you filled Earth with creatures.

27 There is the great sea, broad and massive,
and teeming with countless live creatures,

29 for all of your creatures look to you
to give them their food in due season.

30 When you give them food, then they reap it;
you open your hand, they have good things.

31 When you hide your face they are troubled;
when you take their breath back they perish.

32 You send forth your Spir't, they're created,
you renew the face of the whole earth.

Psalm 105

1 Give thanks to the Lord and proclaim him;
make known all his deeds to the peoples.

9 He knows well his cove-nant with Abr-aham;
the oath that he swore before Isaac,

11 'I'll give to you this land of Canaan;
to be your allotted inheri-tance.'

12 For when they were but few in number;
13 and wand-ering from nation to nation

14 he let no-one hurt or oppress them;
and warned even kings to protect them.

17 Then he sent a young man before them;
this Joseph was sold into sla-very.

23 Thus Is-ra-el came into Egypt,
and Jacob then lived in Ham's homeland.

26 Then he sent them Moses his servant;
and Aaron, the ones he had chosen.

37 God brought out his people with treasure;
38 and Egypt rejoiced when they left there.

44 God gave them the lands of the nations;
they gained all the wealth of the peoples.

Psalm 106

1 Give thanks to the Lord, he is faithful
2 For who can describe his great exploits?

6 Yet we have done wrong like our fathers;
7 who at Egypt's Red Sea were rebels.

8 Yet he rescued them for his name's sake;
9 he scolded the Red Sea, they walked through.

13 But soon they forgot his great wonders;
14 put God to the test in the desert.

19 They made a calf-idol at Horeb
and worshipped a molten-gold image;

20 in this way they exchanged their glory
for some ox that eats hay, a carving.

23 And so he may well have destroyed them,
had Moses not stood there before him,
to turn back his wrath and destruction.

44 Yet many a time he redeemed them,
in malice they dared to defy him;
they were brought low through their wrong-doing.

45 And yet when he heard their distress-cries,
46 Re-mem-bering his bond he had mercy.

48 Lord rescue us too, we shall praise you,
and gather us back from the nations.

Psalm 107.

(This can be sung to the first section of the Mexican hat dance, *El Jarabe Tapatio*).

1 O give thanks to our God, he is gracious,
for his unending love lasts for ever.

4 For then some went astray in the desert;
hungry, thirsty and far from the city.

6 So they cried to the Lord in their trouble
and in all their distress, then he saved them.

10 Some were sat in the dark of death's shadow,
bound in misery from their rebellion,

13 then they cried to the Lord in their trouble
and in all their distress, then he saved them.

23 Some were sailing in ships on the ocean.
They were plying their trade in great waters.

25 At his word the great stormy waves rose up
and they staggered like drunks with no wisdom.

28 Then they cried to the Lord in their trouble,
and in all their distress then he saved them.

31 Let them give thanks to God for his goodness
and the wonders he does for his children.

41 For God raises the poor from their anguish,
42 **and the upright will see with rejoicing.**

Psalm 108

1 My heart it is ready, O God it is ready;
I will sing. I will give you praise.

2 Awake, my soul, wake up! Awake, harp and ly-re,
that I may awaken the dawn.

3 I will give you thanks in the midst of the peoples;
let me hymn you within all realms.

4 Your kindness is great, and as high as the hea-vens;
your faithfulness reaches the clouds.

5 Be raised up, O Lord, high above all the heav'ns;
may your glory light up the earth.

7 In holiness God speaks 'I will divide Shechem,
and share out the vale of Succoth.

8 Gi-le-ad is mine and Manasseh mine also;
Eph-raim my helm, Judah my staff.

9 Mo-ab is my washpot, on Edom I cast shoes,
I'll shout "Tri-umph!" with Phil-i-stia.'

12 O grant us your help Lord against all of our foes,
for earthly help is all in vain.

13 With God as our helper we will do great marvels;
it is he who tramples our foes.

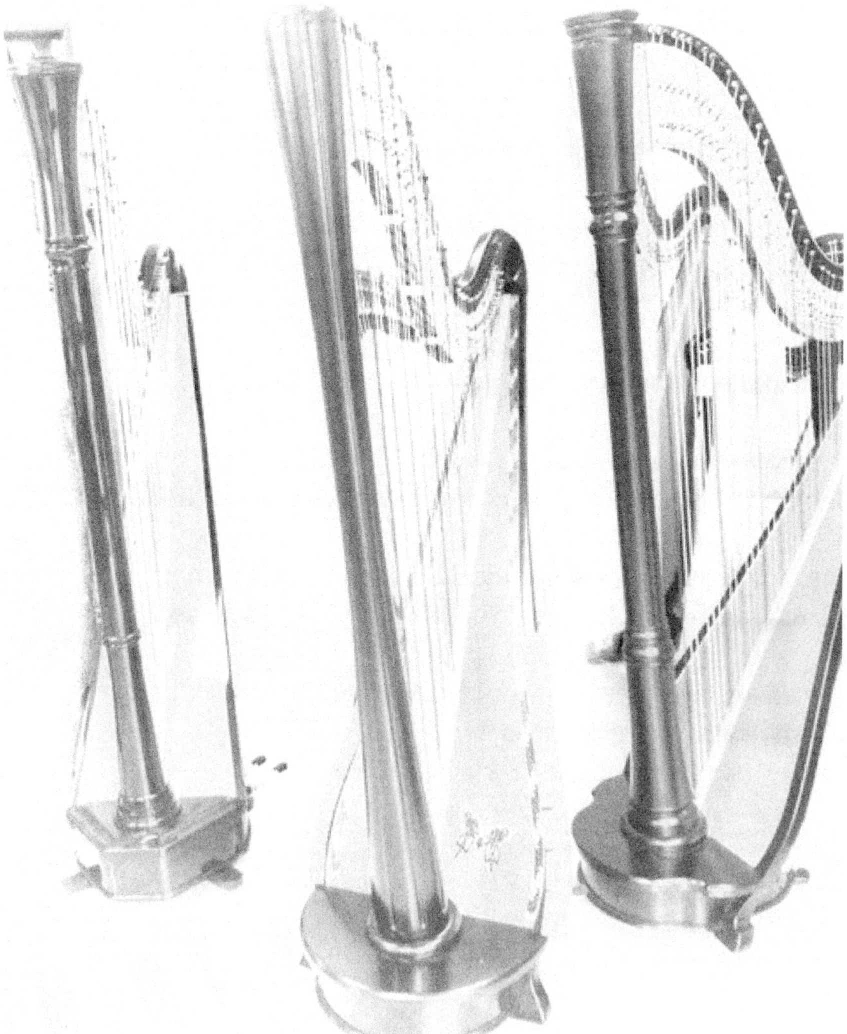

Psalm 109

1 Now keep silent no longer, O God of my praise,
for the mouth of the wicked has opened against me.

2 They have spoken against me with their lying tongues;
they speak their words of hatred, attack me without cause.

3 In return for my love, they accuse me again ;
even though I pray for them, I give myself to prayer.

4 Thus have they paid me back with their evil for good,
at length they curse my life, giving hate for my good will.

20 But now deal with me Lord for the sake of your name;
and save me in your kindness, your faithfulness is sweet.

23 My knees have become weak through my fasting and prayer;
my flesh dried up and wasted.
24 **They shake their heads in scorn.**

25 Help me, O Lord my God; in your mercy save me!
26 They shall know this is your hand; your doing O my God.

27 And though they accuse, me, Lord, I know that you bless;
they will rise, and be shamed, and at that time I'll rejoice.

28 Now let all my accusers be clothed with disgrace;
they will wrap themselves in their great shame as with a cloak.

29 I will give thanks to God in the midst of the crowds;
30 he has stood by the needy to save them all from harm.

Psalm 110

1 The Lord said to my lord, 'Sit at my right hand,
until I make your enemies your footstool.'

2 May our God send forth your sceptre out of Zion;
to rule over your enemies around you.

3 Your people assemble on the battlefield
they offer you themselves in holy worship.

 Arrayed in pure splendour from the womb of dawn
the dew of your new birth is fresh upon you.

4 The Lord God has promised, he will not retract:
'You are a priest for ever as Mel-chize-dek.'

5 The king at your right hand, at your right hand Lord,
shall shatter kings on his great day of anger.

6 In glory he judges nations of the earth;
he smashes heads and piles up all the corpses.

7 He'll drink from the stream that lies beside the way;
And therefore he shall lift his head in vic-tory.

Psalm 111

1 I give thanks to God with all of my heart,
when in the council and in the assembly.

2 The works of the Lord are mighty and great,
they're pondered by all people who desire them.

3 His works are majestic, they're glo-ri-ous;
his righteousness and justice stand forever.

4 He made a me-mor-ial of his great deeds;
our God is gracious and full of compassion.

5 He gives sus-te-nance to those who fear him;
he is forever mindful of his cove-nant.

6 His people are shown the power of his works
in giving them the heritage of nations.

7 The works of his hands are justice and truth;
for trustworthy and true are his commandments.

8 For they will stand firm and strong ever more;
for they are forged in uprightness and God's truth.

9 His people he saved; and made cov-e-nant;
his name is holy and his name is awesome.

10 In fear of the Lord our wisdom begins,
and those who truly know this live by God's words.

Psalm 112

1 How happy are those who honour the Lord,
 who take delight in his commandments.

2 Their offspring shall all be mighty on earth,
 a blest generation of righteous.

3 Great wealth and great treasures shall grace their house,
 their justice will stand firm for ever.

4 Light shines in the dark for these righteous souls;
 they're ge-ne-rous, merciful, blameless.

5 It goes well with those who show grace and lend;
 who honour their words with true justice.

6 They're never perturbed and will never move;
 the good will be always remembered.

7 They will have no fear of any bad news;
 their hearts are firm, trusting in their God.

8 Their heart is sustained, their hearts will not fear;
 until they see their foes defeated.

9 They give to the needy with gene-rous hands;
 their righteous heads lifted with honour.

10 The wicked shall see, and gnash in despair;
 the dreams of the wicked shall perish.

Psalm 113

1 Give praise, you servants of God,
O praise the name of the Lord.

2 Blest be the name of the Lord,
both now and for evermore.

3 From sunrise through to sunset.
praise be the name of the Lord.

4 God rules the empires of earth;
his glory higher than heav'n.

5 Who can be like the Lord God
who has his throne set so high,

yet stoops himself down to view
the things of hea-ven and earth?

6 He lifts the poor from the dust
the needy raised from the ash;

7 he sits them beside a prince,
sat with the most-honoured roy'ls.

8 He gives the childless a home
he brings her children and joy.

Psalm 114

1 When Is-rael came out of Egypt,
   the house of Jacob from strange-tongued tribes,

2 Then Judah became his temple,
   and Is-rael became his sovereign land.

3 The sea saw his pow'r, and bolted;
   the river Jordan was turned right back.

4 The mountains they leapt like young rams,
   the little foothills like dancing lambs.

5 Why was it, O sea, that you fled?
   O Jordan, that you were driven back?

6 Why mountains did you dance like rams?
   O foothills why dance like tiny sheep?

7 Before the Lord your God tremble!
   O earth shake before the Lord your God.

8 Who turns rock into a rock-pool,
   hard flint-stone into a bubbling spring.

Psalm 115

1 Not to us, not to us, Lord,
but to your name give glory,
for your truth and your mercy.

2 Why should those nations taunt us;
they say 'Where is your God now?'

3 Our God, he is in hea-ven;
just what he pleases, he does.

4 Their 'gods' are gold and silver,
from hands of human workers.

5 They have mouths, but they speak not;
eyes have they, but they see not;

6 they have ears, but they hear not;
noses have they, and smell not;

8 may their makers be like them
and all who trust in false gods.

9 Is-rael, trust in the Lord God;
he is their help and their shield.

17 Dead ones don't praise their maker,
nor those gone down to silence;

18 we who live bless the Lord God,
both now and for all ages.

Psalm 116

1 I love the Lord, the Lord my God,
he listens to my desperate pleas;
he bent his ear toward my cries
on the day I called out to him.

2 The cords of death surrounded me;
the pains of hell took hold of me;
I was held by my sorrow's grief.

3 So I called on the Lord my God:
'God I beg you save my life now!'

4 Gracious are you Lord, just and true;
God shows compassion and his love.

5 Our God protects the simple hearts;
I was brought low and he saved me.

6 Once more now rest O troubled soul,
God has now shown his grace to you.

13 Precious within the sight of God
is the death of his faithful ones.

14 O my God I'm your servant too,
and the child of your maid-ser-vant,

16 and I'll fulfil my vows O Lord
in the gaze of the gathered crowds.

17 In the courts of the house of God,
in the heart of Je-ru-sa-lem.

Psalm 117

1 Praise the Lord, all you great nations;
Give him praise, all you his people.

2 God's kindness is great and mighty;
His faithfulness lasts forever.

Hallelujah, hallelujah,
Hallelujah, hallelujah!

Psalm 118

1 Give thanks to the Lord, for he is good;
For his mercy lasts for ever more.

6 With God at my side; I will not fear,
for what can mere flesh then do to me?

7 And with God my saviour, at my side
I'll see all my e-ne-mies fall down.

9 Far better to shelter in the Lord
than put any trust in princes' pow'rs.

10 The armies of nations circled me,
by the name of God I drove them back.

14 The Lord is my strength, God is my song,
and he has become my salvation.

16 The right hand of God does mighty deeds;
God's right hand, it raises us up high.

17 And I shall not die, but I shall live
proclaiming the mighty works of God.

22 The stone which the builders threw away;
that stone has become the cornerstone.

23 For this is the do-ing of the Lord,
and this is a marvel in our eyes.

Psalm 119

1 Bless-éd are those whose path is pure,
who walk in the law of the Lord.

2 Happy are those who keep his words
and with their whole heart seek his face.

5 O that my paths would stay direct
that I might keep all your commands.

18 Unveil my eyes that I might see
the wonders of your precious law.

33 Teach me the way of your commands
and I shall keep them to the end.

34 Grant insight, I will keep your law;
I shall keep it with my whole heart.

49 Recall the words you spoke to me,
on these words you built-up my hope.

50 This consoles me in troubled times,
that your promises bring me life.

105 Your word, to my feet, is a lamp,
it shines a light on my dark path.

128 Therefore I love all your commands;
I love them above finest gold.

Psalm 120

1 When I was in trouble I called to my God;
I called to my God and he answered.

2 Deliver me Lord from the lips that speak lies
and from the tongues that are deceitful.

3 For what can it give you or what can it add?
Deceitful tongues speaking and lying?

4 These lies like the arrows, a warr-i-or's darts,
darts tempered with coals from the broom tree.

5 For woe is me, now I must live in Me-shech
and dwell now in the tents of Ke-dar.

6 I have dwelt too long among those who hate peace,
I've lived far too long among war-riors.

7 I long to make peace and to help med-i-ate
and yet when I speak they make war-plans.

Psalm 121

1 I lift up my eyes to the mountains;
from where then is my help to come?

2 My help it comes from God Almighty,
the maker of hea-ven and earth.

3 The Lord will not let your foot stumble;
he watches you and never sleeps.

4 Behold, he who watches for Is-rael
shall not either slumber nor sleep.

5 Our God himself watches upon you;
the Lord is the shade at your hand.

6 The sun shall not strike in the daytime,
the moon shall not strike you by night.

7 The Lord keeps you safe from all evil;
it's he who keeps guard on your soul.

8 He watches your coming and going,
from this time and for evermore.

Psalm 122

1 I was glad when they said unto me,
'Let us go to the house of the Lord.'

2 And our feet, they can now truly stand
in your gates, O Je-ru-sa-lem town;

3 as a city Jer-u-sa-lem's built
and is bonded together as one.

4 It's to this city that our tribes go,
all the tribes of our Lord and our God.

For this city is where our tribes go
to give thanks to the name of the Lord.

5 For in there are set up judgement thrones,
all the great thrones of King David's house.

6 For the peace of Je-ru-sa-lem pray:
'May they prosper, all those who love you.

7 Let peace be within all of your walls
and tranquility in all your halls.'

8 For my fa-mi-ly and my friends' sakes,
I will pray that peace may be with you.

9 For the sake of the house of the Lord,
I will always seek good things for you.

Psalm 123

1 To you, Lord, I lift up my eyes,
to you Lord who live in the heav'ns.

2 Like the eyes of slaves looking up,
Looking up to their master's hand,

as the eyes of slave-girls look up
Look to see their mistress' hand.

3 So our eyes gaze on the Lord God,
till he pours his mercy on us.

4 O have mercy on us, O Lord,
for we have had too much contempt.

5 Our souls stuffed with scorn from the smug,
filled with such contempt from the proud.

Psalm 124

1 If God himself had not been on our side,
and now may Israel say this;

2 **If God himself had not been on our side,
when people rose against us;**

3 they would have swallowed us whole and alive
when their wrath burned against us;

4 **The waters would all have swept us away;
the flooding passing our necks.**

5 But bless-éd be our great Lord and our God
who has not made us their prey.

6 **Our life escaped like a bird from the hunt;
our traps broke, we were rescued.**

7 Our help is found in the name of our Lord,
who has made earth and hea-ven.

Psalm 125

1 The ones who put their trust in God, are steadfast like Mount Zi-on,
for ever they stand firm.

2 As hills surround Je-ru-sa-lem, so God surrounds his people,
now and for evermore.

3 The weapons of the wicked will not land upon the righteous,
lest they turn and do wrong.

4 Do good Lord, to the righteous ones, to those whose hearts are upright,
to those whose hearts are true.

5 But those whose hearts turn crooked God shall cast off with the wicked;
but Israel shall have peace.

Psalm 126

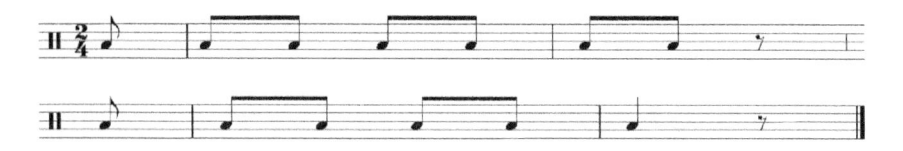

1 When God saved Zion from bondage,
it did seem like a dream.

2 Our mouth was filled with laughter;
on our lips there were songs.

3 They will say to the nations,
'Our God has done great things'

4 God has indeed done marvels,
for this we shall rejoice.

5 Restore us and our fortunes,
as streams within dry land.

6 Those who weep while they're sowing
will sing out when they reap.

7 They go out, full of te-ars,
they bring their seeds to sow.

They come back full of singing,
they come bringing their sheaves.

Psalm 127

1 Unless the Lord God constructs the house,
the builders will labour in vain.

2 Unless the Lord watches over us,
the city guards keep watch in vain.

3 It is in vain that you rush to rise,
and you go so late to your rest.

You eat the bread of your toil and angst
yet he gives his loved ones their sleep.

4 Your children too are a gift from God;
a blessing, the fruit of the womb.

5 Like arrows within a warr-ior's hand
are children, those born in your youth.

6 So happy those ones whose arms are full:
for these ones shall never be shamed.

Psalm 128

1 O happy are those who fear the Lord God,
who fear God and walk in his ways.

2 You shall eat the fruit, the toil of your hands;
for happy and blest you will be.

3 Your wife in your house like a fruitful vine;
your children are like olive trees.

4 Thus shall you be blest, and be blest indeed,
the one who has reve-rence for God.

5 May God always bless you from Zi-on's hill,
may you see Je-ru-sa-lem thrive.

6 And thus may you see your grandchildren thrive,
in Is-ra-el may there be peace.

Psalm 129

1 'Many a time they oppressed me from youth,'
let Israel tell their story;

2 'Many a time they oppressed me from youth,'
they've not prevailed against me.'

3 The ploughers they ploughed their rows on my back;
 they made their furrows long ones.

4 But in God's justice, he has cut me free;
the wicked's bonds he slashes.

5 Let them be turned back in shame who hate Zion;
 let them be shamed and vanquished.

6 Let them be like the green grass on the roof,
which fades before it flowers.

7 With this grass no reaper can fill his hands,
no harvester can gather.

8 And those who pass by, they will never say,
'God's blessings be upon you.'

Psalm 130

1 Out of the depths I cry to you Lord;
O Master hear my voice cry;

and let your ears consider my Lord,
my voice, my cries, my pleading.

2 If you, O Lord, will mark out our guilt,
O God who would survive this?

3 Yet there is true forgiveness with you,
and you shall be re-ve-red.

4 I wait for God, my soul waits for him;
in his words I place my hope.

5 I wait for God, my soul waits for him;
as Night Watch waits for morning.

6 O Isr-ael put your trust in the Lord,
for with God there is mercy.

7 O Is-rael put your trust in the Lord,
in him there is redemption.

He shall redeem, redeem Israel,
from all their guilt and wrong-doing.

Psalm 131

1 O God, my heart is not proud;
my eyes are not haughty and high.

2 Nor have I striven for fame
 with things that are too high for me.

3 But I have calmed down my soul,
like children in their mothers' arms;

like children held on the breast,
so is my soul qui-et in me.

4 O Is-rael, trust in your God,
from this time and for evermore.

Psalm 132

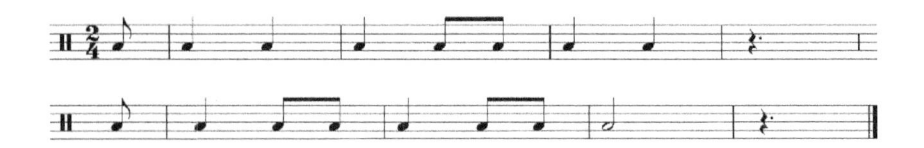

1 O Lord remember for David
the hardships that he has endured.

2 He swore before God Almighty
and vowed before God, Jacob's God:

4 'I won't let my eyelids slumber,
nor let my tired eyes go to sleep,

5 until I find God a dwelling,
to find Jacob's God a new place.'

6 We heard of it in Eph-ra-thah,
and found it in fields of Ja-ar.

8 Come up Lord, come to your dwelling,
both you and the ark of your strength.

9 Your priests shall be clothed with goodness;
your faithful ones they'll sing for joy.

11 The Lord has sworn before David,
a promise that he will not break:

12 'An offspring, fruit of your body
shall I set upon your high throne.'

14 For God has chosen Je-rus-'lem ;
His resting place and his great home.

Psalm 133

1 See how good and pleasant it is;
dwelling like a great fam-ily together.

2 Like a precious oil on the head,
and then running down over the be-ard.

3 Running down upon Aaron's beard,
running down on the neck of his clothing;

4 like the dew, like Mount Hermon's dew
running down on the side of the mountain.

5 There the Lord has promised to bless:
the great blessing of life everlasting.

Psalm 134

1 Come, bless the Lord, all you servants of the Lord,
who stand by night in the temple of the Lord.

2 Lift up your hands to the holy place of God,
and bless the Lord. Bless the Holy name of God.

3 The God who made both the hea-vens and the earth
bless you from Zion, bless you from Jer-u-sa-lem.

Psalm 135

1 Alleluia. Praise the name of the Lord;
give your praise, all you servants of God.

2 All you who stand in the house of the Lord,
in the courts of the house of our God.

6 God does his pleasure in hea-ven and earth,
in the seas and in all of the deeps.

7 He brings up clouds, makes the lightning and rain;
he brings every wind out from his store.

10 He smote the nations and slew mighty kings,
Si-hon of Amor, Og of Bashan.

12 He gave the kingdoms of Caanan away,
a bequest to his people Is-rael.

15 These nations' idols are silver and gold,
they are made by a human's mere hands.

16-17 They have carved mouths, and yet they cannot speak,
and they cannot see, or breathe or hear.

18 All of their makers shall then be like them;
as will all those who trust in false gods.

19 O Is-ra-el bless the name of the Lord,
Aaron's house bless the name of the Lord.

Psalm 136

1 Give thanks to God, our gracious Lord,
for his kindness lasts forever.

2 Give thanks to God, the God of gods,
for his kindness lasts forever.

5 Who by his wisdom made the heav'ns,
for his kindness lasts forever;

6 who laid the earth upon the deep,
for his kindness lasts forever.

Who made the sun to rule the day,
for his kindness lasts forever;

Who made the moon and stars of night,
for his kindness lasts forever.

13-14 Who rescued Isr-ael, parted waves,
for his kindness lasts forever.

17-21 Who smote great kings and gave their lands,
for his kindness lasts forever.

25 Whose goodness feeds all things that live,
for his kindness lasts forever.

26 Give thanks before the God of heav'n,
for his kindness lasts forever.

Psalm 137

1 By Babylon's rivers we sat down and wept,
Yes we wept at mem-ories of Zion.

2 We hung up our harps on a willow tree branch
while our captors asked us for songs.

3 Our captors, they asked us for songs filled with joy,
'Sing us one of your songs from Zion.'

4 But how can we sing any songs of the Lord
whilst we live upon foreign soil?

5 Should I forget you now, O Je-ru-sa-lem,
 may my right hand forget its skill.

6 And may my tongue stick to the roof of my mouth
if Jer-u-sa-lem's memory fades.

If I have not lif-ted Je-ru-sa-lem high
Far high over my highest joy.

7 Remember, O Lord how the Edomites said,
'Cast this town down now to the ground.'

8 Doomed daughter of Babylon, happy the one
who can pay you back for your crimes.

9 Who then takes your little ones as you took us,
takes and dashes them on the rock.

Psalm 138

1 I'll give thanks to you, O God, with my whole heart;
before all the gods will I hymn you.

2 I'll bow to your temple and praise your good name,
because of your truth and your kindness;

for you lifted up your name high over all
and your word is great above all things.

3 The day that I called to you, you answered me;
and you put new strength into my soul.

4 The kings of the earth, they shall praise you, O God,
they have heard the words out of your mouth,

5 and they shall then sing of the ways of the Lord,
that great is the glory of our God.

6 For though God is high, he looks out for the poor;
the lofty he sees from a distance.

7 Though I walk in trouble, you will preserve me;
in spite of my enemies' anger.

you'll stretch out your hand, you will stretch out your hand,
and your right hand it will then save me.

8 For God shall make good his great purpose for me;
**your mercy O God lasts for ever.
Do not leave the work of your hands now.**

Psalm 139

1 O Lord, you have searched me, you know me;
you know when I sit, when I stand;
you see all my thoughts from afar.

2 You mark every path, every rest place;
you're fa-mi-liar with all my ways.

3 There's never a word that my tongue speaks,
that you do not know in advance.

4 Surrounding, behind me, before me,
you set down your palm on my head.

5 Such knowledge is too full of wonder,
too high for my mind to perceive.

6 O where can I go from your spirit?
O where can I run from your face?

7 If I climb to hea-ven, you're with me;
Asleep in the grave, there you are.

8 If I grasp the wings of the morning,
and dwell there beyond the sea's end.

9 Yet there Lord your hand will still lead me,
your right hand shall grasp and hold fast.

12 You fashioned my innermost being;
and knit me in my mother's womb.

13 I thank you, for making me wondrous;
you're mar-vell-ous, and my soul knows.

Psalm 140

1 Save me, O God , from ev-il-d<u>oe</u>rs;
protect me from the vio-lent,

2 who dream up evil in their hearts,
and each day stir up conflict.

3 They edge their mouths like serpents' tongues;
their lips with vipers' venom.

4 Keep me, O God from wicked hands;
protect me from the violent
who seek to make me stumble.

5 Proud-ones have laid a snare for me,
they set their traps on my path;
they spread a net to catch me.

6 I have said 'Lord, you are my God;
O hear my supplication.

8 Don't give the wicked their desires,
Or prosper schemes of evil.'

11 No slanderer shall thrive on earth,
let pitfalls trap the violent.

12 For God will fight the needy cause
and give the poor his justice.

13 Righteous ones will then thank your name,
and dwell within your presence.

Psalm 141

1 Now I call to you Lord; O come quickly to me;
hear my voice when I cry out to you.

2 Let my prayer rise up to you as incense is burned,
my raised hands as the offe-ring at dusk.

3 O my Lord place a watch on the words of my mouth,
place a guard on the door of my lips;

4 may my heart never turn to an evil, wrong thought,
may my heart never join in the acts of the foul,
don't allow me to share in their feasts.

5 Let the righteous correct me and strike me with love;
but the wicked shall not put their oil on my head;
for my prayers are against their foul deeds.

6 Let their rulers be cast down upon stony ground;
they will know then that my words are sweet.

7 As a plough turns the earth, it is parted and split,
so their bones are strewn down in the pit.

8 But my eyes gaze upon you, my Lord and my God;
I take refuge in you; spare my life.

9 From the snare they have laid for me please keep me safe,
keep me safe from the ambush and trap.

10 Let the wicked together fall in their own nets,
while I pass on my way safe and sound.

Psalm 142

1 I cry out to my God; to the Lord I make my pleading.
2 I pour out my complaint and tell God of my distress.

3 When my spi-rit faints in me, I know you show the true path;
in the way where I walk they have laid a trap for me.

4 So I look to my right and I find nobody knows me;
I have no place to run, and no one cares for my soul.

5 I cry out to you, God, I say 'Lord you are my shelter,
you're my portion, my lot, in the living land of love.

6 Listen now to my cry, I have sunk so many fathoms;
save me from my oppressors, they are too strong for me.

7 Bring my soul out of prison, that I may truly thank you;
and the true souls will gather here when they see your gifts.'

Psalm 143

1 Hear my prayer, O my Lord,
faithful God please hear my pleading;
in your goodness answer me.

2 Do not judge your poor slave, do not enter into judgement,
not one living thing is pure.

3 I am crushed to the ground, for my enemy pursues me,
I'm in darkness like the dead.

4 For my spirit is faint, yes my spirit faints within me;
and my heart is desolate.

5 I remember the past; and I think upon your exploits;
all the works of your great hands.

7 Lord make haste, answer me; for my spirit fails within me;
O my Lord don't hide your face.

8 Let me hear of your love, in the morning I will trust you;
O guide me in the right way.

9 Lord I lift up my soul. Save me God from my oppressors,
for I flee towards you now.

10 Teach me how to please you, let your kindly Spirit lead me,
lead me onto level ground.

Psalm 144

1 Bless-ed be the Lord God, the Lord my rock,
he trains my hands for the battle;

3 Lord, O who are mortals that you know them?
humans, that you might think of them?

4 They are like the wind's breath, a puff of wind;
their days like a passing shadow.

5 Bow your heav'ns, O Lord God, and come down soon;
touch the mountains, wrap them in smoke.

6 Cast down bolts of light-ning and part the foe;
shoot your arrows, overpower them.

7 Reach your hand from hea-ven and rescue me;
save me from the mighty waters.

8 They speak words of falsehood and wickedness;
their hands are the hands of li-ars.

9 I will sing a new song to you my God;
playing to you on the harp-strings.

10 You who give sal-va-tion and rescue kings;
from the sword you saved King David.

11 Save me from my fear of the cru-el sword;
free me from the foreign armies.

Psalm 145

1 I will lift you up, my God and my King,
and bless your name throughout all ages.

3 O great is the Lord, most worthy of praise;
his greatness can never be measured.

4 One era shall praise your works to the next
 and proclaim your mar-ve-llous exploits.

5 They'll speak of your glory, your majesty,
and tell of the wonders of your deeds.

10 For all of your works, they praise you, O Lord,
your faithful true servants will bless you.

11 They tell of the glory of your great reign
and speak of your infinite po-wer.

15 The Lord will lift up all those who fall down;
he raises up those who are bowed down.

16 The eyes of all wait upon you O Lord,
you give them their food in due season.

17 Your ge-ne-rous hand is now open wide,
you fill all things living with plenty.

18 The Lord God is true, and just in his ways
 and faithful in all of his actions.

Psalm 146

1 Praise the Lord, O my soul: while I live I praise the Lord;
I will sing praise to God, with my every breath.

2 Do not trust pow'r or princes there is no help in them.
3 When their living breath dies, they return to dust.

4 Happy, those ones who have Jacob's God to be their help,
and who place all their hope in the true Lord, God;

5 who made heav'n, who made earth, the deep sea and all within;
who will keep all his promises ever more;

6 who gives justice to plaintiffs and bread to hungry mouths.
7 The Lord frees all the pris-oners; and heals blind eyes;

8-9 God lifts up those bowed down; lifts the orphans and bereaved;
the Lord loves all the righteous; the good, just souls.

9 The Lord God watches over the strangers in the land;
but the way of the wicked is twisted up.

10 Our God shall reign forever, forever praise his name,
your great God reigns, O Zi-on, for ever more.

Psalm 147

1 How good to make music to our God,
what joy to honour him with praise.

2 The Lord God builds up Je-ru-sa-lem
and gathers Israel's outcasts in.

3 He heals all the brokenhearted ones
and binds up all their weeping wounds.

4 He counts up the number of the stars
and calls each one by their own name.

5 For great is our God, with mighty pow'r;
his wisdom is beyond all speech.

6 The Lord will lift up the low and poor,
but casts the wicked to the ground.

7 O sing to the Lord and give him thanks;
make music to him on the harp;

8 who covers the skies above with clouds
and makes rain for the thirsty earth;

9 who makes grasses grow on mountain slopes
and all green plants to serve our needs.

10 He gives all the hungry beasts their food;
he feeds young ravens when they cry.

Psalm 148

1 Praise the Lord from the hea-vens;
praise him from all the heights.

2 Praise him, all of you angels;
praise him, heav-en-ly host.

3 Praise him, sunshine and moonbeam;
praise him, stars filled with light.

5-6 God called, they are created,
 standing firm evermore.

7 Praise the Lord through the whole earth,
sea monsters, ocean depths,

8 Fire and hail, snow and drizzle,
windstorm on his command.

10 Wild beasts, tame beasts, and cattle,
creeping things, flying birds.

11 Kings of earth and all peoples,
princes, rulers of earth;

12 Young and old, men and women;
may they praise our God's name.

13 His name only is mighty;
splendour in heav'n and earth.

Psalm 149

1 Make music to God, sing a new song;
sing his praise in worshipping crowds.

2 Let Israel rejoice in its maker;
Zion's children have joy in their king.

3 Let them praise his name with their dancing;
let them sing with timbrel and lyre.

4 For our God delights in his people;
with salvation he clothes the poor.

5 The faithful delight in their glory;
and sing out for joy on their beds.

6 The beauty of God's praise in their mouths
and their two-edged sword in their hands;

7 They will seek God's vengeance on nations
and punish the tribes for their wrongs;

8 to bind up their kings in strong fetters,
their nobles with chains made of iron;

9 To execute God's chosen justice:
such honour his servants will have.

Psalm 150

1 Praise God in his holy place;
praise him with his mighty sky-clouds.

2 Praise him for his mighty acts;
praise him for his glor-ious grandeur.

3 Praise him with the trumpet blast;
praise him with harp, lute and ly-re.

4 Praise him with the drums and dance;
praise him on the strings and pipe blasts.

5 Praise him with the cymbal crash;
praise him on the clashing cymbals.

6 Every creature that has breath
Let them praise God. Alleluia!

ABOUT THE AUTHOR

Sue Wallace has been working in music, liturgy and creative worship since the early 1990s when she was the leader of *Visions*, an Emerging Church attached to St Michael-le-Belfrey in York. She has been using musical settings of the psalms since she first sang in a church choir as a small child. Sue is the author of the best-selling Multi-Sensory Prayer series of books which were originally published by Scripture Union and she has degrees in Education, Theology, and also in Liturgy. In 2010 Sue became Team Vicar and Precentor at Leeds Minster and in 2014 she became Canon Precentor and Sacrist at Winchester Cathedral for five years. In 2019 Sue began working for the Transcendence trust which focuses on doing liturgical training and support for those leading traditional worship, and also those involved in Fresh Expressions of church. Her musical tastes are varied. Sue sings and plays the harp and djembe but also enjoys writing and listening to electronic music.

Printed in Great Britain
by Amazon